GOLF
DREAMING

GOLF DREAMING

An Aboriginal Social, Political, Cultural and Historical Perspective of Golf

JOHN MAYNARD

FAIRPLAY
PUBLISHING

First published in 2025 by Fair Play Publishing

PO Box 4101, Balgowlah Heights, NSW 2093, Australia

www.fairplaypublishing.com.au

ISBN: 978-1-923236-24-0
ISBN: 978-1-923236-25-7 (ePub)

Design and typesetting by Leslie Priestley

Except where otherwise stated, photographs are via
Jean-Geoffroy Nyon, John Maynard, and Alamy.

All inquiries should be made to the Publisher via hello@fairplaypublishing.com.au

NATIONAL
LIBRARY
OF AUSTRALIA

A catalogue record of this book is available from the National Library of Australia.

Contents

Contents

Dedication

This book is dedicated to the memory of Anselm John Delaney 1934 – 2024 – J.D. No one represents the Aboriginal connection to golf more than the Gamilaroi legend Johnny Delaney. He was club captain, committee member and a life member of Dunheved Golf Club in Sydney, and he played an instrumental role in establishing the National Aboriginal Golf Tournament in 1979. I was honoured to speak at his birthday in late 2023 and later interviewed him and had a round of golf at Dunheved Golf Club. J.D. was a master storyteller, and we had some great laughs and fun during that round, which I will never forget. J.D will be greatly missed, but his memory and legacy will forever remain to inspire future generations of young Aboriginal people and golfers. Rest in peace, champion.

Foreword

It gives me great pleasure to write the Foreword for this book *Golf Dreaming*. John Maynard has delivered an insight to the passion, attraction and stories embedded in Aboriginal golf. Historically, golf has been an elitist sport only open to people of privilege and self-deluded class, but people such as Charlie Sifford who was the first black American to play on the PGA circuit, Lee Trevino, the happy Mex, Robert Lee Elder – the first black American to play at the Masters, Calvin Peete, Notah Begay III (Navajo), Harold Varner III and of course Tiger Woods, who turned the golfing world on its head and completely shattered the proverbial golfing glass ceiling. Up until 1960 the PGA of America had a Caucasian (whites)-only membership clause and Charlie Sifford, inspired by Jackie Robinson who broke the colour bar in baseball in 1946, set himself the same goal in golf. He achieved his goal in 1961 when he became a member of the US PGA, wiping out the whites-only clause.

Interestingly, golf is a favourite sport with an ever-increasing number of Indigenous people and whenever I meet with brothers and sisters from other nations, we always find our way to a golf course to network and enjoy each other's company. Golf is always on the World Indigenous Peoples Conference on Education (WIPCE) agenda every three years. I firmly believe one day there will be an Indigenous world number one.

From this you will glean that I am a golf tragic. I have loved the game since the first time I had the opportunity to hold a club, which was when I was in my late teens and early 20s. When my daughter Bianca was little, I would take her with me to the golf course and she would run around playing in the bush, and the bunkers, and when she got tired, she would get on the golf buggy and ride for a few holes. A dad and his daughter sharing time and creating memories.

It's ironic that golf would become a passion of mine because where I was born and during my youth, Aboriginal people weren't allowed to join or use the golf club, so we settled for other family-orientated games such as rounders. I have wonderful memories of games of rounders played on the banks of the Namoi River where we lived in our humpies (shacks). Cousins and other kids, even some white kids, would join us for the family fun days and the game of rounders was always run by my maternal grandmother who was totally blind. But her blindness wasn't a hindrance to her because Granny was the boss, and she made all the decisions and made sure that everyone enjoyed the day. Granny would award the 'winners' boiled lollies and everyone had their share and no kid, or adults, ever missed out; an act no doubt to teach all of us lessons about life and the gift of family and kin.

As with so many other Aboriginal people born and raised in the days of the Aboriginal Protection/Welfare Board, we knew what it was to be 'managed' by the welfare officer, and poverty and bigotry were constants in our lives even though as kids we didn't fully understand their poison. Thankfully, times and attitudes change but there's still a lot that remains to be done before we can truthfully say that we live today in a just and civil society.

Along with AFL legend Syd Jackson, Dan Rose and that Gamilaroi legend John Delaney, we created the National Aboriginal Golf Tournament that was first held at Dunheved Golf Club in 1979. Today the tournament is circulated throughout the States and Territories, and it is still going strong after all these years. The tournament has helped to develop several talented Indigenous golfers, some of whom have gone on to be scratch – good enough to be a professional – or low handicappers. Golf has provided the opportunity to share moments of laughter and friendship with special mates, Indigenous and non-Indigenous, throughout the years.

Over the years, I've had the opportunity to play courses I've only ever dreamt of. I've played many, many courses in Australia but my favourite is Bonville, just outside Coffs Harbour. I've also enjoyed rounds at many other courses throughout the country, and I think that I've teed it up in every State and Territory except Tasmania. I've also had the opportunity to play some great courses in other parts of the world – Aotearoa, Hawaii, Canada and the US. My favourite overseas course is Pebble Beach which I've played five times over the years, once with my mates Graham Smith and Rob Tierney and his son Shaun, who sadly passed a little while ago, and another time with Rob, another mate Morrie Black Eagle and his mates from Silverdale/Seattle. The course is everything it is reported to be and the last time we played it was a picture-perfect day. We also played Spy Glass and Spanish Bay during that visit. We stayed at Spanish Bay and during dinner one night, in walked Mark Wahlberg who had played the course just a few groups behind us.

Coeur D'Alene is one of only a few courses on the planet with a floating green and it sits just behind Pebble Beach on the highlight scale. Naturally, the floating green is a par 3 and after you hit your tee shot, you jump in a little boat that takes you out to the green. If you par the hole, you get a certificate. If you don't par it, I'll leave this up to your imagination. I've played the course a couple of times. The last time was with a few of my Aboriginal mates – Ron Gordon, Bill Kennedy and Blackie Gordon.

On another occasion, after attending the first WIPCE Conference in 1987, my mate Nerida Blair and I decided to make a day trip to Whistler, which is a short drive from Vancouver, and of course I wanted to check out the golf course. However, I never quite made it onto the course because after we pulled up, I noticed Sydney Poitier was just finishing his round so I walked up to him, always been a big fan, and introduced myself. We stood and chatted about the civil rights movement that he was a big player in and other social justice matters. He was very interested in what was happening with Aboriginal people in Australia. It seemed like we chatted for an hour, but it was probably only 5 minutes. Nerida was little help because she was starstruck and totally speechless. After Nerida regained some semblance of composure, we went on to explore Whistler, but she couldn't sit still and I wasn't allowed to talk to her, she was lost in the memory of Poitier. I don't have any photos of Whistler but there are great memories. I did play a round with my mate Rob Tierney on the Jack Nicklaus-designed North Golf Course which is just outside Whistler.

So, coming from the humpies on the banks of the Namoi River just below the old Chinese garden, and even though I was not allowed to play on the old Walgett golf course, or perhaps because of it, I have played some of the most beautiful courses in the world with lifelong friends and colleagues.

I hope people enjoy this book and gain an understanding and appreciation of the rich Aboriginal history and cultural connection with this continent.

Professor Bob Morgan

Conjoint Professor, Wollotuka Institute

Professors Bob Morgan, John Maynard and Graham Smith on the magnificent University of British Columbia golf course in Canada.

Introduction

This book *Golf Dreaming* follows on from my previous Aboriginal sports studies, including the history of Aboriginal jockeys, Aboriginal soccer players and Aboriginal boxers, rugby league and Australian rules football players. All my history work seeks to unearth and reveal the many aspects of missing, obscure and erased Aboriginal history. Our people and the wider community need to recognise these missing histories. This new golfing study is an accumulation of personal memoirs, archival research and recording oral memory and stories.

The ancient and noble game of golf is said to have originated in the Scottish Highlands. A game with a rich history and one originally frowned upon by the Crown and authorities, it eventually became the pastime of Kings, Queens and the aristocracy. Then, for a good period of history, it was looked upon as a game only for the wealthy and privileged – back in the 1930s, famed African American scholar W.E.B. Du Bois recognised golf's 'ties to global imperialism, particularly the British Empire.'[1]

In Sierra Leone, Du Bois was incensed that the white community was carving out beautiful English suburbs complete with tennis courts and golf links 'that insulated them from Africans'.[2]

---

[1] Lane Demos (2017) *Game of Privilege – An African American History of Golf,* The University of North Carolina Press, Chapel Hill: 205

[2] Ibid.

Chinese golf chuiwan.

There are claims that the game of golf had its origins in the Netherlands with the Dutch game *kolven* or *kolf*. Another northern European game, *chole*, has also been pitched as the original source of golf. Both games did involve a club and ball being struck and date from at least the 15th century. There was also a very early similar game played in China called *chuiwan*. There have been other speculations on the origins of golf. As early as 1801, Joseph Strutt put forward the idea that golf may have had links to an ancient Roman game played with a feather-filled ball called *paganica*. It has also been speculated that the game may have been brought to Britain by Julius Cesar during his occupation. There have been a host of other claims that have included a Palestinian game called *kora*, the Persian game of *chogan*, a French game called *jeu de mail*. There have even been Egyptian art works that depicted a stick and ball game captured in the tomb of Khety at Beni Hasan dating back to 2000 BC. There is a similar Greek artwork on a marble sculpture from 520-500 BC depicting a ball and stick game.[3] There has even been a suggestion that a form of golf was being played in ancient Chile.[4]

However, in his classic 1892 book *The Art of Golf*, Sir Walter Simpson dismisses all arguments and declared (tongue in cheek) that the Scottish game evolved from a simple discovery by a lonely, bored shepherd who amused himself by hitting a rock with his crook into a series of rabbit holes. With greater substance, while not entirely dismissing other claims, is the conclusion of Neil Millar:

> There is evidence that the game of golf took root in Scotland around the beginning of the sixteenth century, where subsequently it flourished, turning into the modern-day game of golf, a sport that is now truly global. While historians will continue to argue that games played in various countries may have played a part in the early pre-history of golf, many will be satisfied that the evidence is sufficient to conclude that, at least in its critical formative years, golf can be considered to have been Scotland's game.[5]

It is unquestioned that from a humble start, the game flourished in Scotland from the sixteenth century. The Scots were also responsible for transporting the game across the globe from the seventeenth and eighteenth centuries. Certainly, the first reference or mention of golf is recorded in King James VII's Scottish Act of Parliament on 6 March 1457. The Act itself was to ban recreational sports like football and golf. These sports had become increasingly

---

[3] Millar, N.S. (2022) Early Golf – Royal Myths and Ancient Histories, Edinburgh University Press, Edinburgh, p. 174-175

[4] Frezier M (1716) Relation du Voyage de la Mer du Sud aux Côtes du Chily et du Pérou fait pendant les années 1712, 1713 et 1714, Jean-Geoffroy Nyon, Paris

[5] Millar, N.S. (2022) Early Golf – Royal Myths and Ancient Histories, Edinburgh University Press, Edinburgh, pg. 194

popular, and the thought is that King James VII was wary of war with England and wanted his people to concentrate on military sports training, in particular archery which was decreed as compulsory alongside the ban of golf and football.

One royal, King James VII, banned the game, while another, Mary Queen of Scots, later was reputedly roundly criticised for playing golf only days following the murder of her husband Lord Darnley in 1567. Mary herself and the Earl of Bothwell were suspects in the murder. Adding to the suspicion, Mary and Bothwell married only three months after Darnley's murder. Mary Queen of Scots has often been recorded as the first woman golfer. However, Neil S. Millar, in his recent book *Early Golf – Royal Myths and Ancient Histories*, has dismissed the numerous claims of the significant influence of Mary Queen of Scots on the early history of the game in Scotland. Millar reveals that Mary's impact on the game is made on 'exaggerations that are based on a single historical document of questionable reliability'.[6]

Despite the myths, stories and debates on its origins, the game was quickly established as a Scottish national sport. The appeal of the game to all classes has been recorded:

> The greatest and the wisest of the land were to be seen on the Links of Leith mingling freely with the humblest... in pursuit of their common and beloved amusement. All distinctions of rank were levelled by the joyous spirit of the game. Lords of sessions and cobblers, knights, baronets and tailors might be seen contesting for the palm of superior dexterity, and vehemently but good-humouredly discussing moot points of the game as they arose in the course of play.[7]

The game ultimately conquered the globe and would rival soccer for its global participation and impact.

---

[6] Millar (2022), pg. 1

[7] Pollard (1964), pg. 117

In his 1964 book *Gregory's Australian Guide to Golf,* Jack Pollard revealed the impact and spread of the game globally:

> Every year millions of the human race, white, black and red, Slavs, Serbs,
> Japanese, Aztecs, Zulus, Filipinos, Aboriginals, Scots, Cajuns, Mexicans
> and Eskimos, poor men and rich men, old men and very young men,
> white women and Asian women, artisans and professors, match their
> proficiency in swinging clubs against cunningly laid-out courses. In all
> the world, there is probably no game so brimful of legend, ritual and
> superstition as in golf. Australians are rather proud to be among the
> more enslaved of all the peoples golf has ensnared.[8]

The game was introduced to Australia in the mid-nineteenth century. There are several claims for the earliest forms of golf played in Australia. One that can be backed up by archival evidence is ten entries in the diary of Alexander Brodie Spark in 1839. Spark by all accounts was a much respected and connected member of colonial society in Sydney. The diary entries reveal that golf was played in Sydney in 1839 at Grose Farm. Spark and some friends instituted the New South Wales Golf Club on 1 June 1839. But apparently the club had a very short history and disappeared from the records. Nevertheless, the NSW Golf Club (no connection to the present NSWGC) and Grose Farm are the first recognised golf club and course in Australia. Apparently, the golf at Grose Park was influenced through connections with Royal Blackheath Golf Club in England.[9]

In Victoria, golf was reputedly first played on Melbourne's Flagstaff Hill in 1847. It was apparently introduced by the Hon. James Graham, a recent arrival to the colony from Fife in Scotland. Graham had packed a set of golf clubs and "featheries" (feathers compressed into bull hide as balls) in his luggage. He carried a deep love of the game and set up a club that ran for a few years,

---

[8] Pollard (1964), pg. 117

[9] https://en.wikipedia.org/wiki/Golf_in_Australia

but the discovery of gold set off a stampede to the gold fields and all thoughts of the "Royal and Ancient" game disappeared for some time. [10]

Back in NSW, one John Dunsmore, another Scot, brought his love of the game to Australia. He is said to have hit golf balls around on a paddock at Concord in 1851. Despite his attempts, he did not have any success in encouraging interest amongst the locals and had to ditch his idea and hopes of forming a golf club. [11]

In South Australia, the game took off in 1869 when the Governor of South Australia, Sir James Ferguson, established the first golf club in Adelaide. The course consisted of nine holes and was set up near the present day Victoria Park racecourse. The Governor was able to spark an interest in the game and the club quickly comprised 20 active members. The attire of the golfers, consisting of knickerbockers, red coats and tam o'shanters ("tammies" or traditional Scottish caps), was responsible for drawing crowds to watch them in action on the course. However, there was one major obstacle to the course and the golfers, and that was the grazing cattle frequently wandering onto and over the course. The cattle left their hoof marks on the greens and are said to have frequently chewed up the flags on them. Sadly, the cows won the day and the constant damage to the course witnessed the club being disbanded in 1875. [12]

It is recorded that golf was played in Queensland as early as 1880. Again, it was through Scottish influence. Two Scots named Ivory set out a course of a few holes on their cattle station at Eidsvold. The Brisbane Golf Club was formed in 1890. The first course was over nine holes at Chelmer. Only six years later, a full 18 hole course was built at Yeerongpilly. [13]

---

[10] Pollard, J (1964) *Gregory's Guide to Australian Golf (2nd Edition)*, Kenmure Press, Sydney: pg. 126.

[11] Ibid.

[12] Pollard, J (1990) *Australian Golf*, Angus & Robertson, Sydney: Pg. 282-283; Cox, A.B. (1981) Links with a Past - *A history of Golf at Glenelg*, Pagel Production, Glenelg: Pg.10-11.

[13] Pollard, J (1964) *Gregory's Guide to Australian Golf* (2nd Edition), Kenmure Press, Sydney: pg. 127

Early golf and ladies at Ratho Farm.

In Western Australia, the Perth Golf Club was established in 1895 with a nine hole course on Burswood Island on the Swan River. The location was changed several times over the years, during which the Royal title was granted. The WA Golf Association formed in 1910 with the Perth, Fremantle and Cottesloe clubs coming together.[14]

Despite the claims that Alexander Brodie Spark in 1839 in Sydney was the first Australian golfer, Tasmania may well be the birth site of Australian golf. Ratho Farm was founded by Scottish settlers back in 1822. There are claims that local Scottish farmers were playing golf on makeshift courses not long after. The pioneering Reid family laid out the course in 1822 after emigrating from Scotland. The Reid family history relates that they were establishing the golf course at a time when the sport had yet to establish itself outside its original

---

[14] Pollard, J (1964) *Gregory's Guide to Australian Golf* (2nd Edition), Kenmure Press, Sydney: pg. 127.

base in eastern Scotland, from where they and other local families originated. Ratho Farm is unquestionably Australia's oldest golf course, and the oldest remaining outside of Scotland. The course is said to be 'a time capsule, among the best preserved of all the world's early golf courses. Its most apparent uniqueness is the sheep, which graze and keep the playing areas short, with fences to keep them from the square greens'.[15]

Women's involvement with golf in Australia goes back a long way. It is noted that Dame Eadith Walker's Yaralla Estate at Concord was the first venue of 'what was to become the Royal Sydney Golf Club'. Dame Eadith apparently hosted gatherings for games of croquet – 'an appropriate feminine sport'. Eventually, after relocating to Rose Bay, Royal Sydney began:

> life as a golf club for men and a croquet club for women, who, as females, could not be 'full' members: women remained 'associates' of men. The term 'associates' for women golfers has endured for over a century, and for longer in Australia than in any other country.[16]

From these humble beginnings, golf had clearly captured a place in Australian sporting tradition and would produce many world-class golfers in the decades ahead.

---

[15] https://rathofarm.com/golf-course-history/

[16] Douglas Booth and Colin Tatz (2000) One-Eyed – A View of Australian Sport, Allen & Unwin, Sydney, pg. 63

A Personal Golf Reflection

Growing up in the Newcastle suburb of Adamstown was an introduction to my lifelong love of sport. A lot of time was spent at the local racecourse at Broadmeadow with my father, a top jockey. At the back of our home and only three blocks away was the Merewether Golf Club. The club was established in 1933 and as a young boy I and a number of other kids would haunt the Merewether course during summer. We would spend our time swimming in the club's dams and retrieving golf balls. We also hunted through the surrounding bush and scrub for wayward balls and would be back up at the clubhouse selling our collection of cleaned-up balls to the golfers for a tidy little return.

As a young teenager, I began to play the game just for fun over at the Broadmeadow Racecourse, where they had a golf course in the centre of the racecourse. It was a rough and ready course, but great fun. The Newcastle Jockey Club Golf Course originally opened in 1933.[17]

My jockey father earned a riding contract in Singapore and Malaysia during the early 1960s. It was over in the east that my father and mother took up the game of golf. I remember the beautiful wooden Bobby Jones Jnr clubs and irons in the green golf bag that hung in our garage after the return from Singapore. They did not continue playing golf once they were home and that was why the clubs were hung in the garage.

I was the one that brought them out of mothballs and put them in the little fold-down green buggy. I wheeled them down to the racecourse links and was hitting and whacking my way around with a baseball grip. I had never had a

---

[17] Newcastle Morning Herald and Miner's Advocate, 11 September 1933: 8

Merv Maynard riding winners in Singapore 1961-1964.

lesson but found the game fun. I played with my cousin Gary Middleton, and I once managed to coax my father out of his golf retirement to have a hit. I recall that my father had a beautiful swing and made the game look simple.

One incident has stayed in my mind over many years from playing at the racecourse. I was on a tee that faced away from the inside track of the racecourse, known as "the cinders" and used for early morning trackwork. I recall teeing up the ball and looking down the fairway. To the right of my vision was a tractor coming along the cinders. I swung back and connected with the ball, and it fairly flew off the club with a zing. But it sliced to the right and was travelling at great speed towards the tractor driver. It all happened in a split second, but his head went down like a tortoise into its shell and the ball flew where his head had been. The guy came up, shook his head and drove on.

I can recall going out and having a hit in my late teens and early twenties with mates and girls riding around in golf carts and having a few beers along the way. But I had a long layoff from the game when I spent most of the 1970s and early 1980s living and working in England. I first landed in London after working as an on-flight groom looking after million-dollar racehorses flying to England from Australia.

On my return home, I did take a great interest in watching the golf majors during the 1980s, probably driven by Greg Norman. I watched Norman on telly win two British Opens, but he was also denied on so many occasions by just bad luck and freakish shots from opposing players. Who could ever forget Larry Mize chipping in from off the green in the 1987 United States Masters. The greatest tragedy was still ahead when going in with a six-shot lead over long-time rival Nick Faldo in the 1996 Masters, Greg Norman completely imploded on the last day. It remains as one of the most heartbreaking sporting collapses I have ever watched.

During the late 1980s, I started to dabble with the game again after an old friend, Michael Dwyer, had returned to Newcastle to take over as commander of the Hamilton Army Reserve Barracks. Mick had a long career in the army as a paratrooper of some note. I remember him appearing on 60 Minutes being interviewed by Ray Martin over several parachute jump school deaths around Western Sydney. Mick had returned to Newcastle because after years of parachute jumping, his knees were shot and that was why he gained the position as commanding officer at the Hamilton Barracks. He decided to take up golf and joined Charlestown Golf Club. He encouraged me to join as well.

We only played against each other. He would pick me up and we would head out for a round. I remember one day coming up the seventeenth hole and the sky was an angry blue/black. A major storm was threatening to erupt. I just said to Mick, 'That's it for me, I am heading to the club'. Mick insisted, 'Come on, there is only one hole to go.' I said, 'No chance,' and set off up the hill. I heard him grumbling following behind me. No sooner had we got there and picked up our beers than there was this massive thunderclap, and from the clubhouse window we saw a bolt of lightning strike a large gum tree on the eighteenth hole. A great sheet of fire and smoke went up from the tree. Mick looked at me and said, 'Ok, you were right.'

On another occasion, Mick had received an invitation for the opening of Cypress Lakes Golf Club in the Hunter Valley, due to his position with the army. It was a special invitation tournament for the opening and Mick got me to go along with him. We both had big handicaps and won a section of that tournament, winning gear and dinners as I recall, and I still retain my Cypress Lakes cap from that day.

Around this time, I started studying at university. I remember during my years in the Diploma entry course, my late Auntie Marie (my grandmother's sister) being so excited that I was going to university. She had been a great supporter through my young life, and she had invited me down to stay with her at her home at Lake Macquarie for a couple of weeks. She would cook great meals for me, and I had access to her great library. She wanted me to have time and a place to both relax and study in a good environment. She really spoiled me over that time. She was one person right across my young life who insisted I should go to university. While I was staying there with her, I realised the 1994 Australian Open was on the next weekend. I decided to catch a train down from Morisset Station to Central and head out to Royal Sydney Golf Club to watch the likes of Greg Norman, Wayne Grady, Mark Calcavecchia, Robert Allenby, Brett Ogle and Craig Parry battle it out for the title.

Robert Allenby won the Open by a shot from Brett Ogle with Greg Norman three shots back. Watching that tournament at Royal Sydney was thrilling and exciting, and to watch Greg Norman up close at the peak of his powers was something to behold. I recall a shot where he must have been a hundred and seventy yards back down the fairway firing into an elevated, large green. I thought when he hit it that it would be too big, but it smacked down right up at the back of the green and for a split second stopped stationary, then suddenly as if on an elastic band, it shot back down the green to stop inches from the hole. That was backspin at an extreme level. As part of my day, I wandered around the course and came across a large Heineken beer marquee with Heineken beer girls added for good measure to promote the brew. I stopped and asked one of them what the marquee was in aid of and whether you could get in. She replied, 'No it is a private corporate function'. I said, 'Too bad, it looks like a fun event'. She looked at me, reached down and plucked up a Heineken golf hat, handed it to me and said: 'But I will invite you in'. I still have that Heineken golf hat.

During my studies and after, I was employed at the University of Newcastle's Wollotuka Institute variously as a research assistant, associate lecturer, research officer, research academic and eventual director. During those years at Wollotuka, golf again returned to my radar. Wollotuka colleague and friend Fred Maher and I established the Wollotuka Golf Club where we and some of the other staff members and students would play a round of golf as a social get-together. We played in and around Newcastle at courses like Charlestown, Morisset, Belmont, Maitland, Toronto, Kurri and Shortland Waters. It was just for fun and a good get-together. Some of those involved in those days included Joe Perry, John Shipp, David Button, Ray Kelly and Bud Kelly, to name just a few.

When Laurel Williams was director at Wollotuka, she requested that Joe Perry and I conduct some research for her at Dungog Historical Society. I cannot recall what she sent us up there looking for, but I do recall Joe saying as we left her office: 'I will pick you up in the university car and bring your golf clubs'. Well, we did the research and gathered the material requested, then we set off to the Dungog Golf Club. It was a good day until we reached a short par three over a small dam. I lined up and proceeded to hit every ball I had in my bag into the dam. Joe started rolling balls over to me from his bag until

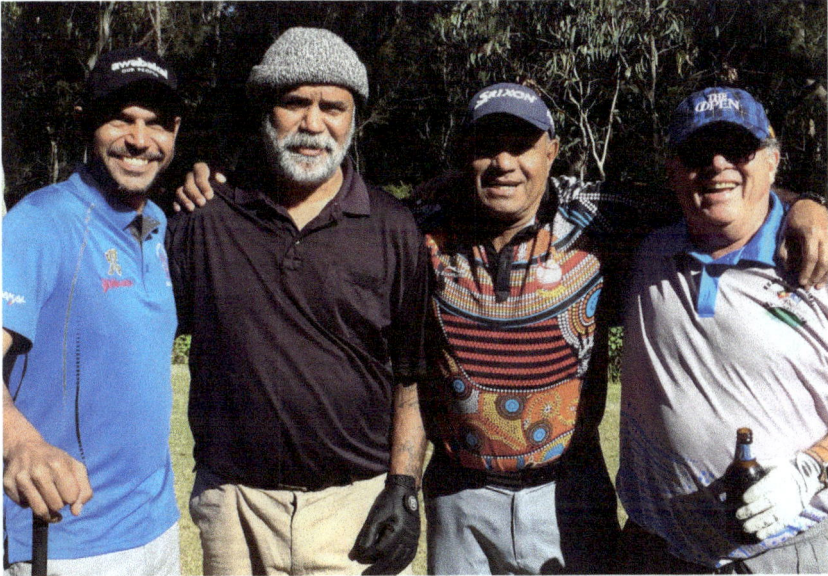

Wollotuka Golf Club – Bud Kelly, Ray Kelly, Joe Perry and John Maynard.

I exhausted his supply. While this was going on, a guy over the other side on a tractor stopped to watch us and wait before he proceeded with his work. As Joe Perry has told me many times over the years: 'That guy nearly fell off the tractor he was pissing himself laughing so much'. Our golf day was over at Dungog.

Joe and I played every now and then at courses like Merewether, Maitland and Tanilba Bay, sometimes with a slab on the back of the cart. Brother Trevor Patten would sometimes join us. Trev was such a character and has now sadly passed away after a long battle with cancer. I remember one day we were all playing up at Maitland and discussions were about the pairs sharing golf carts. At that moment, Trevor Patten turned up 'badly burned' and looking the worse for wear from a big night out. Joe Perry, as always, was quick off the mark. He looked at me and said, 'You've got Trevor.' I still laugh at the thought, as at one point Trev was lying under a tap he had turned on to run over his face. He then had a white towel wrapped around his head looking like Lawrence of Arabia as he climbed into the cart. But when I drove off, Trev fell out of the cart!

In the mid-1990s, I spent two years working for the Indigenous Health Unit

John Maynard with Worimi bro Joe Perry

as a research officer in the Faculty of Health Sciences at the University of Newcastle, undertaking a major national study *Healing Our Way*. This project aimed to gain a grassroots Aboriginal perspective on not just health issues but also cultural and historical issues that non-Indigenous medical professionals and students need to be aware of when coming in to work with Aboriginal peoples and communities for the first time. The project's scope encompassed all sections of the national Aboriginal community, including urban, rural and remote locations. I worked on this project with a young brother from Dubbo, John Shipp, over two years. We had opportunities to meet and interview so many significant senior Aboriginal people across the course of the project.

During our off times over the course of those two years, John and I would unwind on the golf course. We frequently bet twenty bucks on the longest drive. We played in Central Australia, Broome, Kempsey, Perth, Crescent Heads and

Adelaide. One of the funniest memories of that period was when we played at West Beach in Adelaide. John stepped up and smoked a drive straight down the centre of the fairway. He turned around laughing and roaring, 'Match that.' I stepped up and smacked it, and it sliced to the right straight over the fence and hit the road outside. John said, 'You owe me twenty bucks.' I said, 'Get stuffed, you owe *me* twenty bucks. Look at that thing, it's still going down the road heading to Glenelg. It's a mile past yours!'

The Wollotuka Golf club fell into a period of non-activity for a while. But we continued to catch up with the local Newcastle NAIDOC Week golf event which was always a big day for us. The Awabakal Golf Day held during NAIDOC Week was always a great day. One year it was held at Merewether golf course. I was teeing off on the hole facing up the hill adjacent to the army barracks to its right. We could see the group ahead along the fairway out of my range, and there were some large trees on the right along the fence. I let fly and the ball for once sizzled and took off with a zing. At that exact moment, Warwick Thompson stepped out from among the trees looking for a wayward ball. My ball cracked into his head, and he went down like he had been hit by one of his dad's (former Commonwealth boxing champion Hector Thompson's) left hooks. There is nothing more sickening than hitting someone with a golf ball. Warwick was transported by golf cart up to the clubhouse and I went up and visited him lying on a lounge in the club. He said, 'Brother what happened, what hit me?' I didn't have the heart to say it was me.

The Awabakal Golf Day later became the Jimmy Wright Classic Golf Day after his passing and it was held at Jimmy's old course at Charlestown. Jimmy Wright was a prominent member of the Newcastle community and a former ATSIC Commissioner over many years. He was always a mover and a shaker who could get things rolling.

In 2012, I was fortunate enough to win the Newcastle Awabakal C-Grade Golf Championship, and in 2013 I followed that up by taking out the NSW State Aboriginal C-Grade Championship. The State titles that year were played at the Crowne Plaza Golf Resort at Pokolbin in the Hunter Valley vineyards.

There were also international trips through conference presentations,

John Maynard with bro Ray Kelly and his grandson Bilum Henry at the Jimmy Wright golf day.

research grants and invitations to visit and speak. In 2006, during my time as director of the Wollotuka Institute of Aboriginal Studies, Professor Bob Morgan and I underwent a long trip to Canada and the United States. The trip was about consolidating our international contacts and connections, looking for areas of collaboration and at what other international Indigenous centres were doing at the time.

Our journey would take us from one side of Canada starting at Vancouver to

The late Dr Mary Young and her husband Ron with John Maynard on the course in Winnipeg.

the other side, visiting Halifax and just about everywhere in between, as well as a visit across the border to North Dakota to visit Standing Rock Reservation and Sitting Bull College.

During our travels, Bob and I played a couple of rounds of golf with First Nations' scholars and academic colleagues. We played a round with the late Dr Mary Young and her husband Ron in Winnipeg. At the University of British Columbia (UBC) in Vancouver, we played on the magnificent UBC course. Only just prior to our visit, it had hosted the Canadian Junior Championship. It was a spectacular pine tree-lined course. Alongside Māori scholar Graham Smith, we were joined by the dean, Rob Tierney, for a round of golf. We also had lunch at the University staff club that overlooked the course. Rob Tierney explained to us that the golf course was a great attraction for Asian students who flocked to enrol with UBC because the course was such a magnet.

This experience encouraged me to investigate creating something similar at the University of Newcastle when I returned home to Australia. Right

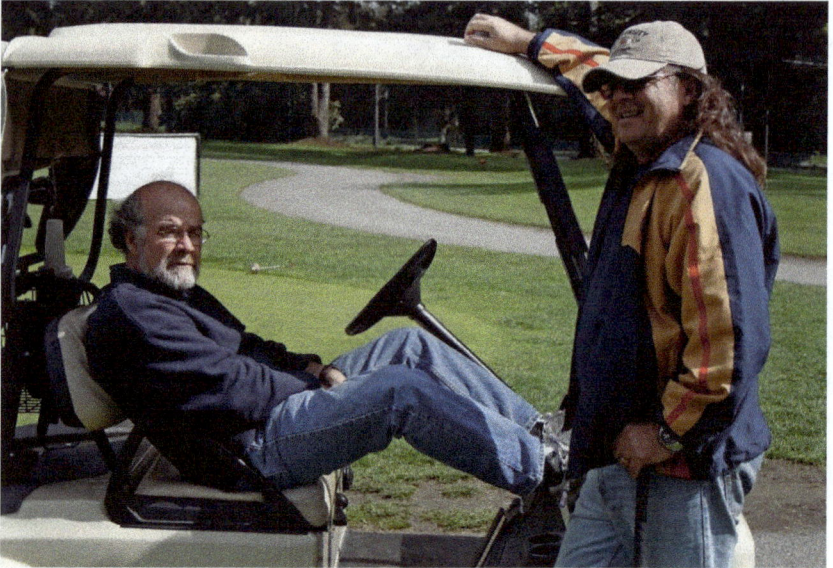

John Maynard and the Dean at the University of British Columbia at the time Rob Tierney.

alongside the University of Newcastle sits the former Broken Hill Proprietary Company (BHP) golf course, now known as Shortland Waters. The university had a connection with the golf course in that two holes on the course were on university land, which has never been a problem. The golf course itself was going through a time of financial duress and falling membership numbers. I had always thought that the university should market itself as the sporting university of Australia and with two visible national football clubs – the Newcastle Knights (rugby league) and Newcastle Jets (soccer) – the city already had a national sporting profile. The university also already had NuSports and was about to establish a major sports science centre at Ourimbah at the time.

I joined Shortland Waters Golf Club and was having a regular round on the course and occasionally going across to the old club for lunch. I arranged to catch up with some of the board members of the club and outline what a great opportunity it would be for the golf club to form a partnership with the university – a win-win outcome for both groups. In my mind, I envisioned a conference centre and accommodation alongside the course, and just like UBC, we could use this to attract Asian students. The golf club would be relieved of financial stress and gain assistance for course upgrades and development. There was such potential! With more than 5,000 staff and over 30,000 students, a marketing strategy could have been developed to encourage this large potential membership group to sign up as members of the golf club.

Sadly, the old members of the committee were up in arms and howling that the university was out to swallow up the golf club. This was complete nonsense, but this did not halt their stampede of opposition. The university vice-chancellor at the time, Nick Saunders, also a keen golfer, had tried the same approach and was also met with fierce resistance to the idea by the Shortland Waters Golf Club. I remember meeting with Nick in his office at the university where we discussed the great potential of the partnership. I still think both the golf club and the university missed such a wonderful opportunity.

Shortland Waters eventually went down the path of a partnership with the Aveo Retirement Group. This saw the construction of new holes and a new clubhouse, but the club's financial woes continued. The course redevelopment took much longer than anticipated. There were many temporary greens in use that resulted in declining membership numbers and placed a severe strain on the clubs' finances. It was realised by 2018 that the board needed to put the club into administration. The club had hoped to find backing to see their way out of financial troubles but had no luck. Later that year, the Aveo Group purchased the golf club completely for $1.8 million dollars and were the new owners. The golf club itself was granted a lease on the course for the next twenty years and they sought and were granted a further additional twenty years lease on the course for just $1 a year rent. This was a survival outcome, but I still feel that the university option would not have seen them lose ownership of their course.

Over the years, I have had many opportunities to play and experience the game in some great locations, courses and events. In 2013, I was overseas in the United States to research Australian Aboriginal and Native American comparative history. I was in Miami, Florida speaking at the 2013 Indigenism, Pan-Indigenism and Cosmovisionism: The Confluence of Indigenous Thought in the Americas Conference. The conference was hosted by the University of Miami. It was exciting to be in Miami, the home of *Miami Vice* and the site of Muhammad Ali's victory over Sonny Liston back in 1964 to become the heavyweight boxing champion of the world.

I had a few free days and wondered what golf courses were close by. I discovered that Doral, known as the 'Blue Monster', was not too far away. It has been owned by Donald Trump's organisation since 2012. The world-renowned course is recognised as a bucket-list golf destination. It is a golfer's haven. First opening its doors in 1962, Doral was built with golf at its core. Visitors discover that it is one of the pre-eminent luxury golf resorts in Florida. I knew that the 'Great White Shark' Greg Norman had won a few events on the course and thought I would try and get a game. I rang up and there were no problems. Out I went for a great day to play on a fantastic course. I could not help but notice that Donald Trump had seemingly put his own stamp on the course. The drink and food carts that regularly called on players during the round were all driven by very attractive, young blonde women. I really enjoyed my round, and I made par on the fourteenth hole par five and that made my day.

In 2015, I was again overseas having been invited to join a group of African American scholars on a Trans-Atlantic Dialogues on Cultural Heritage Conference in Liverpool in the UK. I loved being in Liverpool, visiting Anfield, home of the Reds and once graced by Newcastle footballer Craig Johnston. Also, the Beatles! I went on a Beatles bus tour of the city, including all the major sights like Strawberry Fields, Penny Lane and the Cavern Club.

But there was a very big golf highlight to this Liverpool trip. I noticed that the British Open was being held at St Andrews in Scotland, and due to tee-off on the Thursday. I had already given my talk, and I had a free day on Thursday. I went to Lime Street Station at Liverpool and enquired how I would go about catching a train to St Andrews. I was informed that to get there the next morning around 10:00 am, I would need to catch a train around 5:30 am in the morning. That was no problem to me and the next morning I set off on a great train ride to Edinburgh, transferring to another train through to Leuchars on the northeast coast of Fife. There was a switch from train to bus for the final leg to St Andrews.

I had a sensational day as I followed the group that consisted of Tiger Woods, Jason Day and Louis Oosthuizen. In front, I also watched Jordan Spieth and eventual winner Zach Johnson. I just had the time of my life that day. The weather conditions on that opening Thursday were sensational for golf – blue sky and sunshine, and not a hint of wind. I witnessed some incredible golf, drank a few cold beers, and snacked on fish and chips and a magnificent roast pork roll. I got away towards the end of the day, catching the bus back to Leuchars and the train back to Liverpool. It was a long day, and I don't think I got back until 5am in the morning, but it was worth every minute.

In 2016, a four-year research project examining the missing history of

John Maynard at St Andrews for the British Open in 2015.
Even up close to Tiger Woods.

Aboriginal military service was coming to its culmination. I was down to speak on a panel presentation about our project at a big Indigenous Studies conference held in Honolulu in Hawaii. My wife Vicky and I decided to take a family holiday just prior to the conference starting. We took our two youngest boys with us to Hawaii, and we stayed at the Aulani Disney Resort on O'ahu. It's a truly beautiful location with lagoons, pools, water rides and slides, and a beautiful beachfront. Vicky and I just sat back sipping cocktails while the boys, then aged ten and twelve, tore about the place. Directly opposite was the Ko Olina Golf Club, so I had the opportunity to have a crack at a course regarded by *Golf Digest* as one of the 'Top 75 Resort Courses in the U.S'. It was built in 1990 by renowned golf course architect Ted Robinson. Typical of his designs, Ko Olina Golf Club features exceptional water features, multi-tiered greens, large landing areas, and it's a moderate length which makes it perfect for beginners and experts alike. It proved a challenging but enjoyable 18-hole course.

In 2017, Vicky was awarded a Fellowship in London. I took our youngest sons, Kaiyu and Kirrin-Yurra, over for a visit. Our eldest son, Ganur, was studying in Europe at the time and we all gathered in Paris to celebrate Vicky's 50th birthday. We also went out and stayed at the Disneyland Paris theme park at Marne-la-Vallée, west of Paris. The complex includes a Disney-themed golf course. Popular with adult visitors, and just a few kilometres from the theme park is Golf Paris Val d'Europe, known as Golf Disneyland. I went along during our stay for a round over the eighteen-hole course and managed to par a couple of holes. It's a very nice course.

In 2019, we had another Disney-themed family holiday to Disney World in Orlando, Florida. It was a fantastic holiday. Our youngest boys were now old enough to be let free on their own and Vicky and I had a relaxing holiday. Our older boy, Ganur, was back in Sydney starting his career as a lawyer. Golf was also on my agenda at Disney World and there are four top courses, including the Arnold Palmer course, Lake Buena Vista. This classic country-club style course winds through pastel villas, pine forests, palmettos and sparkling lakes. Lake Buena Vista has hosted the PGA Tour, the LPGA Tour and USGA events. I really enjoyed Lake Buena Vista and it is up there as one of the best courses I have played.

I first had the opportunity to join the Newcastle Golf Club in 2017. Newcastle has long been regarded as one of the best kept secrets of Australian golf courses and for many years was rated in the top twenty courses in the country. I had joined the Newcastle Jets as a Gold Card member and one of the perks of that season was that you could join the Newcastle Golf Club for a much reduced rate. Newcastle Golf Club is an Australian gem. I was working at the time and only played the course once a week. It was around this time that I developed serious knee problems and had to stop playing, but I retained my membership as a non-playing member at Newcastle.

I was also plagued with other major health issues around this time. In early

2018, I had knee replacement surgery and only a month following, suffered a heart attack and had a stent inserted. There was a slow rehabilitation and physio period over the year, but I recovered my health and was back walking and beginning to feel much better.

The heart attack was bad enough, but then the pandemic erupted in Wuhan, China, in late 2019. It quickly spread globally and in no time had hit Australia. We had long lockdowns and chaos, fright and confusion. It is just so surreal looking back on this period. We had a long period of time just working from home and I took to being a reclusive, anti-social hermit. I liked doing a Zoom meeting or writing some stuff, then sitting out the back of the house with a coffee talking to the beagle. When the dust finally settled on COVID, the University of Newcastle offered some staff the opportunity to take a payout to leave or retire. Initially after nearly thirty years connected to Wollotuka and so many good friends, it was a hard decision, but then I just said 'No, that's it, I'm out.' I took the package, and my superannuation was able to be taken as an indexed pension and that was it. I was retired.

I had recovered from my knee operation and was feeling much more mobile, so I decided to reward myself by re-joining Newcastle Golf Club. Having held a previous membership prior to my knee problems, I was reinstated. I started playing by myself just for fun. It is such a great course. One day I was joined by a big lanky Scot, Gordon McLeod. A retired electrical contractor, Gordon was a dyed-in-the-wool Glasgow Rangers and Liverpool supporter which made for some good old-fashioned rivalry and sarcastic comments between us both, with me being a Celtic and Manchester United supporter.

We had a lot of laughs and fun. Occasionally, someone else would put their name down with us, but they never came back for more. We laughed that one game with us was enough for anyone. On one occasion however, we were joined by a retired German chef, Reinhold Forster. We gave him the nickname Rhino and he also enjoyed the game and a laugh, so we were a trio. I was later contacted by another old friend from the University of Newcastle, Paul Scott. Paul was another who loved the game of golf but could see the funny side of things and never let the game become too serious. We were along for the ride of a game and a good laugh. Over the past four years, we have also ventured away from Newcastle and played at courses like New South Wales, Royal Canberra, The Lakes, Bonville, Cypress Lakes, Horizons, Magenta Shores, Bonnie Doon, Hawks Nest, Elanora and Pacific Dunes. We had also joined both the Sydney Veterans Golfers' Association and Travelers Golf Club, which provided access to so many other top courses.

In mid-2023, my wife Vicky also joined and was happy to play once or twice a week. We decided to have a weekend away every now and then either at Port Stephens or the Hunter Valley Vineyards, having a round of golf and sampling some great food and wine. In late 2023, we decided on a three-week vacation in Britain when Vicky took long service leave. Over the past twenty years, we have had many trips overseas to conferences to give talks and conduct research, but they were always for work. On this trip, it would be just a holiday, and we scheduled some golf as well. We went to London, Cornwall, Liverpool and Scotland, and after my opportunity to visit the 2015 British Open at St Andrews, it was on the top of my bucket list.

We caught the train from London to Lytham St Annes, a seaside location

Fun at St Andrews with Victoria Haskins 2023

south of Blackpool. With my Newcastle Golf Club membership, we had a reciprocal connection with St Annes Old Links course at Lytham St Annes. We arrived late at night having booked into the Grand Hotel right on the sea. The following morning, we trekked around to the course on a very bleak and overcast day. The big surprise was that the club did not have a golf club hire facility, but the pro shop guy managed to scrape a bag together and was able to get us a buggy. We enjoyed our round in wild conditions. It was still richly rewarding to play the course and have a few drinks at the clubhouse after our round.

The major golf focus of the trip was spending five days at St Andrews. We had caught the train up from Kings Cross via Edinburgh. We were booked into the Old Course Hotel – a magnificent hotel that overlooks St Andrews golf course. The accommodation was superb, and we had dinner the first night at the Road Hole restaurant overlooking the course and followed up with a Scotch-tasting session in the bar. I was in the draw to play St Andrews through the Hotel but also had another chance through advice from a Scottish academic friend. I just had my fingers crossed. Meanwhile Vicky and I were booked by the hotel to play the Duke's Course, high above St Andrews with spectacular views of the coast. It was designed by legendary Australian golfer Peter Thomson, a five-time winner of the Open Championship (British Open). The hotel catered for everything, even organising a van and driver to take us to the Duke's and return later to pick us up. It was a beautiful day. We did not light up the course, but we had a great day. We later walked around St Andrews visiting the golf shops and historical sites. It's such an interesting place.

My hopes for a game on the Old Course came up trumps on Thursday 11th October. But after all the great weather we had experienced, Britain was hit by a major storm named Babet. It was cyclonic in intensity, with pouring rain and wind clocked at over 70 mph. I was convinced that my chance to play St Andrews was over, but when I checked with the golf desk at the hotel, I was informed that the course had not been closed and was in fact booked out. The hotel thankfully would drive me up to pick up my hire clubs, then on to the starters' office next to the first hole. I was told that I would be teeing off at 11am. The office was packed with keen golfers, but the noise of the storm and its intensity was visible to all within. There was no time for a warm-up or practice putt, and, in all honesty, I had no desire to be out there early. It was quite cold, and I had a few nips of scotch to warm the innards. I was finally told to head to the first tee to join three Americans, a father and son and another lone player like me.

On the first hole, known as "the Burn", I hit a wayward shot out to the left, blown there in the gale force wind. I managed to extricate myself from the rough and drove it over the Swilken Burn but way to the back, it was impossible to control the ball in the gale and rain. The golf buggy would also often take off or just tip over due to the force of the wind. I fared a little better on the second and third holes. The American father and son thought the better part of valour was heading back to the starters' hut. So, me and the big lanky Yank plodded on, and it appeared that the weather had even intensified. I drove the ball away well on several occasions with such a gale behind me, but I could not see where it ended up. Visibility was down to a minimum. Eventually, I had to take my glasses off to see a little bit better.

My best moment was on the eighth hole. I drove the ball wayward out to the right into heavy gorse-like scrub but managed to find it. I then fired a high shot into the air that came down ten yards from the hole. It was very difficult to putt in the wind. The ball was always jumping about and trying to move off, but I managed to shave the hole and tapped in for a four. Under those weather conditions, I believe that my four on that hole was the greatest bogey I have ever scored.

I scored a six on the ninth hole known as "the End". This was the location of the halfway house, and I bought another little bottle of scotch and nipped into it to try and gain some warmth. Although I was wearing wet weather gear, I was soaked through to the skin and freezing. The fellow at the halfway house informed us that we were only one of two groups still playing the course. All the others had given up. I realised that it was madness to continue, and a cart had just arrived that would drop me back at the club hire shop. So, I ran the white flag up and headed off the course and back to the hotel for a hot bath and more whisky. It took me hours to thaw out, but a nice dinner overlooking the course in the wild storm with a lobster entrée and a beautiful lemon sole main course had me on the mend.

It was a thrill playing St Andrews in that storm. I will never forget that just getting to play this famous course was a once-in-a-lifetime moment. Vicky and I then had a stressful and hair-raising trip back to London as the roads and train lines were cut. There were long delays, but we eventually made it and were finally boarding the plane back to Sydney. The trip to Britain and playing St Andrews is my final reflection of my own personal golf experiences which now stretch back over sixty years. But what about the game, our history with golf and what it means to Aboriginal people in this country?

An Aboriginal Sporting Tradition and Missing History

Modern golf was played in Australia from the very early days of the nineteenth century. However, there were forms of golf played in Australia thousands of years ago. While today golf is a popular pastime for many Aboriginal people (which is surprising in itself), very few people realise the historical connections between Aboriginal people and Scotland's royal and ancient game of golf.

Aboriginal culture was a sporting culture. Aboriginal people played traditional games that were all about teaching skills, building athleticism and stamina, which were integral to a hunting and gathering lifestyle. These games were taught and encouraged from a very young age. Anthropologist Herbert Basedow compared the Aboriginal focus on strict principles of sporting behaviour to the regimentation of the Spartans of ancient Greece.[18] Missionary Lancelot Threlkeld noted in 1834 that Aboriginal people of the Newcastle and Lake Macquarie region of New South Wales were encouraged to practise sporting contests and games from a very young age: 'children practice, in sport, the attack and defence, using a piece of bark of a gum tree for a shield, and small grass stems for spear'.[19] Convict artist Joseph Lycett captured the strict discipline incorporated by Aboriginal people in their sporting pursuits. These sporting contests captured the fitness and practised skills of the Aboriginal participants: 'The sporting games were obviously much enjoyed by all members of the tribal

---

[18]   Basedow, 1925:87

[19]   Gunson 1974:68

group – in Lycett's image, women and children are sitting on the side-lines cheering on their favourite participants.'[20]

There are countless early settler accounts and observations of the physical health and fitness of Aboriginal people across the country. My own people, the Worimi of New South Wales, were recorded and noted for their health and imposing physical attributes: 'some of the blacks were nearly 7ft tall'.[21] An observer of the Aboriginal people of Coal River (Newcastle) in 1827   remarked upon their imposing physical presence: 'You seldom see a black under five feet eight or nine inches. I have seen them about six foot four in height.'[22] Robert Dawson at Port Stephens observed the agility and speed of the local Worimi people: 'they go up the largest and tallest tree with great facility' and noted 'their quickness is astonishing'.[23] Aboriginal people played forms of football, most famously a game in Victoria called marngrook that many claim is the origin of today's popular Australian rules football game. But the precedents for golf haven't been explored before.

In the late nineteenth century anthropologist and Queensland protector of Aborigines Walter E. Roth recorded in his studies in Queensland that Aboriginal people 'played a sort of golf but without clubs. There was only one hole, and that was a pit, guarded by a cross bunker in the form of a net.'[24] The game involved throwing a bone 'from a prodigious distance, and to hole in one'.[25] Roth recorded another throwing ball game that was played 'with a leather ball, bound with hard twine, not vastly different in its component parts from the earliest golf balls'.[26] Roth revealed another game involving a boomerang that was not about making it come back but instead to make it 'fall directly on an agreed spot

---

[20]   Maynard, 2014:60

[21]   Clayton 1952:4

[22]   *Newcastle Morning Herald*, 11 May 1993

[23]   Dawson 1830:68

[24]   *Register News*, Adelaide 1929: 7

[25]   Ibid.

[26]   *Register News*, Adelaide 1929: 7

marked with a peg in the ground', a target much like a golf flag on the green.[27] Another version of an Aboriginal golf game was recorded in Victoria:

> They played a game that looked like golf, but which they called 'witch-a-witch'. Shaping a knob of wood like a long hen's egg, they split it at one end, and fastened therein a piece of stick from the prickly bush and made soft by working in the ashes. This handle was about 18 in. long, and when everything was ready the young men would gather and choose a suitable piece of ground. They would then swing the contrivance over their heads striking it on the ground in a sloping direction. If the stroke were well executed the 'witchie' would rebound to a height of about 20ft, shooting like a comet for about 200 to 300 yards. After each had had his throw, the lot would wander about like golfers, looking for their 'witchies'. When they were found they would repeat the performance.[28]

After the British arrival in 1788, Aboriginal people suffered horrifically, and such traditional games fell into disuse. Economic historian Noel Butlin estimated during the 1980s that the Australian Aboriginal population was decimated by somewhere between 60% to 90% through a combination of violence, disease and depleted resources only six decades after the British arrival in 1788.[29]

Throughout the nineteenth and twentieth centuries, in addition to the many disadvantages that Aboriginal people endured, colour bars of exclusion stopped Aboriginal participation in many sports. Top Aboriginal sportsmen and sportswomen were denied the chance to play at the highest levels that their talents deserved. It was not until the 1960s, a time of great social and political upheaval globally, that Aboriginal people began to break through into the sporting arena, with the likes of world bantamweight boxing champion Lionel

---

[27] *Register News*, Adelaide 1929: 7

[28] *Australasian (Melbourne)*, 1944:30

[29] Butlin, N (1983) *Our Original Aggression*, Allen & Unwin, Sydney: 175.

Rose and seven-time tennis Grand Slam singles tournament winner, Evonne Goolagong Cawley. The decade witnessed the floodgates opening and over the past fifty years, a flood of Aboriginal AFL and rugby league stars burst on the scene. The period culminated with Cathy Freeman's dominating performance at the 2000 Olympic games in Sydney, winning gold in the 400 metres final.

Golf was perhaps one of the most difficult sports for Aboriginal people to break into. For a good period of its history, and even today, the sport was looked upon as a class-conscious game only for the wealthy and privileged. This made it a difficult game for the greater part of the twentieth century for Aboriginal people to take part in, as golf clubs were expensive, and one needed to gain admission to a golf club to play.

There were certainly barriers to Aboriginal participation with the game or even gaining access to a golf course. As Colin Tatz insightfully directed:

Golf has hardly been within the Aboriginal grasp. Group 1 courses – those deemed worthy of holding championships – have annual dues of between $2,500 and $5,000 and joining fees can be three to four times that sum; and in 2017 a reasonably good set of clubs and accessories was in the vicinity of $2,5000 and closer to $3,500 for the best quality.[30]

Wray Vamplew and Brian Stoddart acknowledged in their social history study on Australian sport that Aboriginal participation in golf suffered due to all the 'usual structural reasons', including financial barriers for equipment, club membership, practice facilities and genuine role models, but concluded that 'an abiding theme must also be that of rejection based on colour and cultural lines'.[31]

But Aboriginal people were innovative in finding ways and means to play the game. Many were confined and enclosed on tightly restricted government

---

[30] Tatz, C & Tatz, P (2018) *Black Pearls – The Aboriginal and islander Sports Hall of Fame,* Aboriginal Studies Press, Canberra: 23

[31] Vamplew, W & Stoddart, B (1994) *Sport in Australia a Social History,* Cambridge University Press, Cambridge: Pg. 89.

A foursome walking down the fairway at Wallaga Lakes in 1936.

Aboriginal reserves and missions during the first half of the twentieth century. These reserves controlled every aspect of Aboriginal life including diet, clothing, housing, movement and even dictating who people could marry.

However, in 1936, the Yuin Aboriginal community on the south coast of New South Wales did something different. With the support of the mission manager who was clearly a golf lover, they built their own golf course on the Aboriginal reserve at Wallaga Lake. The course consisted of five holes and 'not only did the Aborigines construct the course with its perfect greens, but they have also fashioned their own clubs from wild cherry and hickory saplings'. Several of the Aboriginal players were expert players, with two of them having scored a hole in one on the course. A 'prominent member of the Royal Sydney Golf Club at Rose Bay, who has seen the Wallaga Lakes course, considers it the most picturesque in Australia.' A newspaper article that year described its beauty:

Driving off from the first tee at Wallaga Lakes in 1936.

[From] the greens one looks down on the placid Wallaga Lakes, which teem with fish and black swans, while blue mountains complete a perfect picture... Those boys are living in paradise.[32]

The golf course and the support for Aboriginal players disappeared after the manager was moved on. The golf course fell into disrepair and eventually disappeared from memory. Such descriptions obscure the darker history of violence and dispossession that is a major feature of Australian history. Golf courses were created on First Nations' country with little if any respect for the wishes of the people whose country it was. Aboriginal golf participation is for the greater part of history one of exclusion from the game in this country. There are no substantial records of Aboriginal players gaining access to mainstream courses before the 1960s.

---

[32] *Nowra Leader,* 1936: 4; *Smiths Weekly,* 1936: 4.

Golf Courses with Aboriginal Sites of Significance

There are many Australian golf courses today that have sites of deep Aboriginal cultural significance within their properties. A number of these courses promote that relationship and seek to protect these sites, while others are totally unaware of the Aboriginal presence at all.

The Bondi Golf Club was built in 1935 and is near one of the most famous beaches in the world. It offers spectacular views of the coastline. The course is also a great spot to view whales on their migration journeys along the east coast of Australia between May and November. The club draws attention to the fact that the course holds Aboriginal rock carvings on the fifth hole.

The whale holds a special and significant relationship with Aboriginal people. On a major rock carving section of Bondi Golf Course, a sign directs you 'that the central figure is a whale about twenty five feet long, the head of which has weathered away; within and near this whale is cut a porpoise, a large fish and a shark, each about eight feet long... Just beyond where the head of the whale would be, there is a large figure about thirteen feet long, cut diagonally across the group; it has a man-like shape, but a long tail below this figure inclines the writer to think that it was a compound figure, part man and part iguana. There is a much weathered small or deity close to it, and on its western side is a large circular blubber with a large fish and boomerang cut within it.'[33] The engravings were noted by a Mr. W. D. Campbell as being 'all much weathered'. In 1894, they were so badly eroded 70 years later that, in an attempt 'to preserve their outlines', they became the first (but not the last) Aboriginal rock carvings in Australia to be "officially' regrooved'.[34]

---

[33]   Rhodes J (2018) *Cage of Ghosts*, Darkwood, Hong Kong: 132

[34]   Ibid: 130

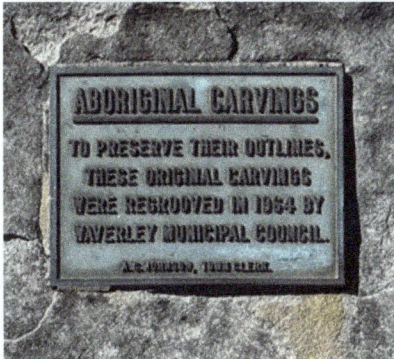

The magnificent Aboriginal rock art site on Bondi Golf Club. The plaque reads: "Aboriginal Carvings To preserve their outlines, these original carvings were regrooved in 1964 by Waverly Municipal Council A. C. Johnson, Town Clerk."

Writer Jon Rhodes in 2007 was able to speak to the man who had supervised the regrooving. He explained that the figures engraved on the 'southernmost rock, about 50 feet in length, were probably of an older date' than the figures on the northern rocks, as those outlines had been 'cut broader and deeper'. These 17 carvings included 'a seal with a shark and a large fish cut transversely over it in reverse positions... a few feet northward there is a schnapper and a boomerang, and beyond these, a large fish possibly a shark, and three other smaller fish partly weathered away'.[35]

At La Perouse, there are also rock engravings on the ocean coastal edge of the golf course, and the headland. The carving of a whale and calf explains the Dreaming story of Buriburi, the humpback whale. The designs were created by joining a series of pecked holes to form the outlined figures and were sometimes later re-cut, as they eroded away. Some engravings were used as teaching places, while others were places of ceremony.[36]

The Buriburi engraving site also highlights the important link of the sea to coastal Aboriginal people. 'Fishing and collecting shellfish were certainly central food gathering activities, but fishing was also woven into culture. It featured in engravings, fish hooks, shells and personal adornments made from fish jaws'.[37] These remarkable carvings near the golf course remain as a record and testimony to the richness of life before the invasion in 1788. Coastal Aboriginal people of south-eastern Australia lived in a virtual paradise of plenty, and the rich and varied resources available sustained large populations of people. As an example of the bountiful Aboriginal marine environment, James Cook observed that at an Aboriginal camp at Kamay 'there were small fires and fresh mussels broiling upon them; here likewise lay vast heaps of the largest oyster shells I ever saw'.[38]

An important area of contention is over the actual size of the Aboriginal

[35] Rhodes J (2018) *Cage of Ghosts*, Darkwood, Hong Kong: 132

[36] Walker, A & Irish P (2023) *Golf on Gamay*, New South Wales Golf Club Foundation, Sydney: 11.

[37] Ibid: 12

[38] Fitzsimmons, 2019: 292

population of Australia in 1788. Butlin has quoted Governor Phillip estimating that the Aboriginal population was over 1 million people.[39] In May 1788, Phillip noted: 'It is not possible to determine with any accuracy the number of the natives, but I think in Botany Bay, Port Jackson, Broken Bay, and the intermediate coast they cannot be less than one thousand five hundred.' On 9 July, he expressed with some concern that the 'natives are far more numerous than they were supposed to be'. He also stated that he had seen smoke inland estimated at fifty miles distant and 'leaves no doubt… that they are inhabitants in the interior part of the country'.

The next day, he confirmed his estimate of a population of fifteen hundred 'natives' confined to within just a ten-mile radius of the settlement. During the 1930s, anthropologist Radcliff Brown made an estimate of 300,000 Aboriginal people being on the continent in 1788.[40] This was challenged later by Mulvaney and White with a more realistic appraisal of at least 700,000 people.[41] Economic historian Noel Butlin increased that number to between 1 to 1.5 million Aboriginal people in 1788.[42]

If Butlin was correct, this then raises a question. Where did they go? By the turn of the twentieth century, the Aboriginal population was recorded at just 70,000 people remaining. Butlin was one who had no doubt. He felt that the 'combined effects of disease and resource competition may have reduced black numbers in the course of about 60 years to about 10 per cent of the '1788' level'.[43] Aboriginal people of the area survived this onslaught and although greatly reduced in numbers, lived on into the late nineteenth and twentieth centuries.

It is critically important today to recognise that despite the cataclysmic impact of the British arrival upon Aboriginal Australia, including massive loss of life, we survived. This included ground zero in Sydney and La Perouse. The Aboriginal cultural connection to country continues into the 21st century.

[39]   Butlin, 1983: 5

[40]   Butlin, 1983:5; Butlin, 1993: 99

[41]   Butlin, 1993: 99

[42]   Ibid.

[43]   Butlin 1983: 175

Respected La Perouse Elder Rod Mason, who grew up in the area, refers 'to the cove in behind New South Wales Golf Course as Cruwee Cove or Pussycat. It is an important spot for myself and my family, as we have camped there for generations. We would camp between the 5th and 6th holes when it was windy and access banabi, or fresh water, nearby. While camping there, we fished and dove for fish and shellfish.' [44]

The coast was lined with large middens holding the remains of thousands of years of feasting on fish and, shellfish and land animals:

> that Aboriginal people ate, along with tools of bone, stone, and shell. Around and sometimes within these living places Aboriginal buried their dead. They were sometimes cremated, and other times buried in graves... Aboriginal people continued to be buried immediately east of the golf course into the twentieth century. Due to this practice, the Little Bay cemetery and lands extending south along the eastern edge of the golf course were declared an 'Aboriginal Place' by the NSW Government under the National Parks and Wildlife Act 1974.[45]

The Aboriginal experiences since 1788 are in many instances histories of brutality and suffering. It is well understood that one of the most horrific prisons of Australian history was set up on Rottnest Island off the Western Australian coast near Perth. The island was later converted into a holiday destination including a golf course. There are several burial sites on the island that are believed to hold Aboriginal remains. In 1987, Mr Shardlow, the Rottnest Island building supervisor, revealed 'that graves had been uncovered in May 1962 when a trench was being dug. The bodies had been in rows about 60 centimetres apart and appeared to be buried in the sitting position. The area was cordoned off to curb the curiosity of residents and visitors. We tried to keep the kids away, but the adults were worse. Some even picked up skulls and ran away with them.' [46]

---

[44] Walker, A & Irish P (2023) *Golf on Gamay,* New South Wales Golf Club Foundation, Sydney: 20

[45] Ibid: 14

[46] Green, N & Aguiar, S (2018) *Far from Home – Aboriginal Prisoners of Rottnest Island 1838-1931,* Focus Education Services, Perth: 61

A Mrs Cowie, the lodge housekeeper, claimed that more bones were uncovered with the construction of a fence near what had been the prison infirmary.[47] In 1979, Mr Des Sullivan, the Rottnest Island manager, insisted that graves were uncovered in 1971 when a sewerage scheme was being extended to the golf club.[48] Sullivan went on to remark that the discovery of the burial site was kept secret as the board feared it 'might have encouraged vandals to desecrate the graves'.[49]

It was not until 1985 that Peter Randolph from the Aboriginal Sites Department 'formally recorded the existence of the cemetery and marked its approximate location'.[50] In the 1988 bicentenary year, a large protest meeting on Rottnest Island expressed concern at the neglect of the graves and called on the State government to step in. A ground-penetrating radar (GPR) survey was conducted that established the length of the cemetery and it was finally fenced off and signs erected to inform the wider public of its significance. Disputes have continued over the site and its length, but the Noongar Regional Council in Perth was not willing to undertake any further action because of the sensitivity of the location.[51] The stories of Aboriginal burial sites on Rottnest and its later reincarnation as a tourist and holiday destination are graphically noted:

> This island idyll was also haunted by Rottnest's sombre history: the "dark shadow still cast by the earlier use of the island as an Aboriginal prison". In the 1980s, the island's history was coming to light, and tourists were starting to learn that the "Aboriginal past is also a part of the experience".[52]

---

47   Ibid.

48   Ibid: 62

49   Ibid.

50   Ibid.

51   Green, N & Aguiar, S (2018) *Far from Home – Aboriginal Prisoners of Rottnest Island 1838-1931,* Focus Education Services, Perth: 63

52   Curthoys, A, Koneshi, S & Ludewig, A (2022) The Lives and Legacies of a Carceral Island: A Biographical History of Wadjemup/Rottnest Island, Routledge, London: 370; Seddon, G (1983) "The Rottnest Experience", Journal of the Royal Society of Western Australia, 66, pts 1 and 2: 34

The contrast between Rottnest Island and the North Adelaide Golf Club is clearly visible. The North Adelaide Golf Club has embraced its Aboriginal cultural and historical connections. The golf course sits on Pirltawardli (Possum Park). It is three courses: two 18-hole courses and a par-3 course. The first Christian mission for Aboriginal people in South Australia was established at the site in 1839, only two-and-a-half years after the Europeans had landed at Glenelg. It was built north of the River Torrens, opposite the site that became the Adelaide Gaol. Pirltawardli (meaning possum home) was already a regular camping ground for the Kaurna Aboriginal people of the area.

The original mission was set up by German Lutheran missionaries Christian Teichelmann, Clamor Schürmann and, later, Samuel Klose. The mission was a substantial settlement for some years. At its height, it was a fenced area of 5.7 ha, and together with traditional wurlies (temporary shelters), it contained mud and straw houses for the missionaries, and smaller huts and a school for the Kaurna people. At the insistence of the missionaries, the children were taught in the Kaurna language.

After it closed, the Kaurna people continued to camp near the site. Pirltawardli, also called the 'Aboriginal Location', is now of major significance to Kaurna people and is also important to non-Indigenous South Australians. Nearly all the recorded language and early written records of Kaurna culture stem from this place, documented by Schürmann and his associates, who also recorded their observations of race relations in early Adelaide. Pirltawardli has been revived as the area's official name, and in 2000 a plaque was erected commemorating its place in Adelaide's history.[53] It is a testament to these missionaries that they saw the importance of Aboriginal language that was very rare for any religious group during those early years. The site of the mission right next to the par-3 course is memorialised by several marker stones with images of the Kaurna people and their connection to the site. The main clubhouse of the North Adelaide Golf Club proudly flies the Aboriginal flag as a mark of respect.

---

[53] https://sahistoryhub.history.sa.gov.au/places/pirltawardli

Rottnest Island Burial Marker.

In Queensland, the Keperra Golf Club had its beginning in 1928 as the Enoggera Golf Club on property that was jointly owned by the Catholic archdiocese, and a 'well-known Brisbane journalist, Major General Spencer-Brown'.[54] In 1949, it was reported that the picturesque golf club was to be developed further into a complete sporting club and showpiece only 10 miles from the centre of the city. The article revealed that the golf course was originally 'carved from scrub housing settlements of golden pheasants, whip birds and red fox'.[55] It further highlighted that 'where golfers play now was once the sacred ground of an Aboriginal tribe. There is a Bora ring close to the present clubhouse and golfers have assured the Historical Society they will preserve it.'[56]

It was stated that the club's name was changed to Keperra after the small railway station a few hundred yards from the first tee. This opens an interesting aside with the Bora ground connection. The Aboriginal word Keepara was the

---

[54]   *Brisbane Telegraph,* 10 September 1949: 5

[55]   Ibid.

[56]   Ibid.

Several stones markers highlights aspects of Kaurna history and the North Adelaide Golf Club proudly flies the Aboriginal flag.

The flag of Keperra Golf Club.

ceremony for initiation for Aboriginal boys on their journey to manhood. It is highly likely that the name is tied to Aboriginal ceremony and the location of the Bora ground. In connection to the Keperra Golf Club site, it was later recorded that it was an Aboriginal word referring to a young man or a Bora ring; a large Bora ring was nearly obliterated by earthworks during the construction of the Keperra Golf Club in 1931.[57]

Something must have been retained for the members to inform the Historical Society in 1949 that they would protect the site. Adding weight to this thought is information on the club's website in relation to its club shield that highlights the Aboriginal connections.

In the centre a broad ring (chaplet) coloured white (argent) and decorated with aboriginal designs alludes to the Bora Ring, principal historical feature of the golf course... The crest is a bent (embowed) right arm coloured black (sable) representing an Aboriginal's arm holding a

---

[57] https://queenslandplaces.com.au/keperra

woomera and spear. The woomera, an instrument used to hurl a projectile into the air is a symbolic allusion to the golf clubs, the spear symbolic of the golf ball.[58]

Golf clubs across this country carry deep connection to Aboriginal history and culture. Some clubs are taking advantage of this connection and seeking to work collaboratively with Aboriginal people and communities, and this can only benefit both parties in a very positive way. As an example, the Wolston Park Golf Club on the banks of the Brisbane River applied for and received a government grant to undertake improvements to their course. They used some of the money to add colour to the Halfway Hut that had been dedicated to life member Mary Byrne. The club employed local Aboriginal artist Glen Evans to paint and invigorate what had been an old drab shed into a stunning Aboriginal landscape artwork.[59] These are the sorts of initiatives that golf clubs should explore to develop relationships with their local Aboriginal communities.

---

[58] https://www.keperragolf.com.au/cms/club/history/

[59] Newberry, D (2023) *Inside Golf,* May: 14

The Caddy Connection

In 1988, the year of the Australian bicentenary, a beautiful book *After 200 years - Photographic Essays of Aboriginal and Islander Australians Today* captured the essence of both the La Perouse location and Aboriginal caddying connections to the game of golf. Klein described the contradictions captured in an image depicting:

> An elderly Aboriginal man in a striped shirt is pulling his golf cart along the links at La Perouse, a posh coastal suburb of Sydney. Walking off the 7th tee, his back is turned to Botany Bay and his gaze is fixed firmly on the ball he has just hit. A former caddy at the club, he is playing in the annual Aboriginal Golf Tournament. Ironies abound here: in the setting (the site of Captain Cook's landing); in the game (what symbolizes a privileged Western way of life and use of land better than golf?); and in the fact that this photograph appears in a book published on the occasion of Australia's Bicentenary. [60]

The following 1988 image overleaf captured by local Aboriginal man Peter McKenzie shows Aboriginal golfers Cyril Cooley, Bertie Woodland and Gary Sait playing in the annual La Perouse Aboriginal Golf Tournament.

This chapter explores the experiences of Aboriginal people gaining opportunities to caddy on golf courses. Stories of Aboriginal caddies, while

---

[60] Nadel-Klein, J, (1991) Picturing Aborigines: A Review Essay on After Two Hundred Years: Photographic Essays on Aboriginal and Islander Australians Today, in *Cultural Anthropology*, Volume 6, Issue 3, August 1991: 414-423.

1988 La Perouse Aboriginal Golf Tournament. (Photo: Peter McKenzie)

evenly spread across the continent, were rare in that Aboriginal people were less likely to be in the vicinity of a quality golf course. Nevertheless, some locations did provide opportunities.

As a comparison, there are many historical records of African American golf caddies in the United States. The history of black caddies in the United States is unquestionably tied to the history of slavery. Records reveal that black men were being used as ball finders and caddies in the late nineteenth century. Some of the top African American golfers during the 1930s in the United States 'hailed from rural areas of the south and Midwest, where many used positions as caddies, groundskeepers, and attendants at segregated golf facilities to access the game'.[61] Arguably the most famous golf course in the world, Augusta National Golf Club in Georgia, had a very strict policy on entry and membership from its inception in 1932. It was very blunt in its racially

---

[61] Lane Demos, 2017 *Game of Privilege – An African American History of Golf,* The University of North Carolina Press, Chapel Hill, xi

Aboriginal caddies at the New South Wales Golf Club.
(Photo: Paul Irish, Tony Sernack, Kate Shanks)

segregated 'policy of only employing black caddies... "as long as I'm alive," said Clifford Roberts, who founded the club alongside famed amateur Bobby Jones, "all golfers will be white, and all the caddies will be black."'[62] It is important to recognise that golf 'was an early battleground of the Civil Rights Movement in the United States'.[63]

While black golf caddies, particularly in the south in the United States, were a feature of the golfing world, this was not the case in Australia. There were a few areas where Aboriginal communities were near golf courses and in these rare instances, golf offered Aboriginal people opportunities for

---

[62] Lane Demos, 2017 *Game of Privilege – An African American History of Golf,* The University of North Carolina Press, Chapel Hill: Pg. 77

[63] Kirsch, G.B (2007) Municipal Golf and Civil Rights in the United States, 1910-1965, *The Journal of African American History,* Vol. 92, No. 3 (Summer), pp.371-391; in Ashawnta Jackson, 2022, http://daily.jstor.org/daily-author/ashawnta-jackson/

employment. Aboriginal men acted as paid caddies at golf clubs at places like La Perouse in Sydney and Stuart Island at Nambucca Heads. The caddying experiences of Aboriginal people in Australia range from gross exploitation to innovative enterprise.

La Perouse on the southern beaches of Sydney has a proliferation of golf courses including New South Wales (founded in 1926), St Michaels (1938) and the Coast (1965). Uncle Vic Simms stated strongly: 'Aboriginal football (rugby league) is represented by the blokes from La Perouse and Redfern because there were no other sports. There was no golf. The closest they got to golf was carrying the rich bloke's bags as caddies.'[64] The boys would go 'caddying, carrying rich peoples' golf bags around the courses that prevailed around La Perouse in those days. And then save up and get themselves a pair of shoes (football boots).'[65]

Gloria Ardler recalled as kids that they all 'played in the bush area from Bundy down to La Perouse, up the golf links road to Happy Valley and down to Frog's Hollow and never heard of any one of us getting bitten by spiders or snakes'.[66] Lee-Ann Mason recalled the kids went swimming and diving for money after school at Congwong Beach, La Perouse and Bare Island. She said: 'we girls also picked up golf balls at the Dan Cullen Driving Range to make a bit of pocket money'.[67]

La Perouse Public School Headmaster, Mr W. E. Champion, said in 1947: 'I admire the dark children for their ingenuity. After school many of them earn money by caddying at golf links and by selling boomerangs. Eleven-year-old Norman Longbottom told me he had been selling boomerangs to visiting

[64] Vic Simms, 2021 Jai McCallister – A History of Aboriginal Rugby League in NSW – ABC Radio.

[65] Ibid.

[66] Maria Nugent, 1987 La Perouse – the place, the people and the sea, Aboriginal Studies Press, Canberra.

[67] Ibid.

American sailors for £2 each'.[68]

Each year during NAIDOC Week, Aboriginal people from across the State flocked to La Perouse and competed. Numbers were usually in the vicinity of 150 golfers. Cyril Cooley stated:

> that local Aboriginal people had a long association with the course from caddying on it and working as greenkeepers there. The executives of the golf club always invite us back each year to play and they always make us very welcome. I first went there caddying in 1934. We went caddying because there was no work to be had and we used to get 25 cents to carry the bag around. It was one of the few ways to earn a bit of money in those days.[69]

Respected Elder Noel Timbery has reflected on growing up on La Perouse and the golfing connection:

> I started caddying at New South Wales in the early 1950s. Back then, caddying was the only option to earn an income from the golf course as there was a ranger on horseback who would chase us away if we tried to collect stray balls. I was lucky enough to develop a relationship with a member of New South. He was a local butcher who would play at 1pm on Saturdays and Sunday at around 8:30 am. I caddied for him for a number of years, and I would earn $4-6 a round. I would sometimes caddy for other golfers, and I remember caddying two and half rounds in one day. We had good times, but it was very strict at NSWGC, we weren't allowed near the front of the club and had to go around the back to access the kitchen for food. The other members and I of the La Perouse Aboriginal community who caddied developed a real love of

---

[68] Ibid.

[69] Taylor, P (1988) *After Two Hundred Years: Photographic Essays on Aboriginal and Islander Australians Today,* Aboriginal Studies Press, Canberra: 345

golf. I am left-handed but had to learn to play with my right hand as they were the only clubs we had access to. We would hit balls anywhere from waiting at the tee box while caddying to down at Yarra Oval. We even started Sydney United Golf Club back in 1979 and [had] up to 60 members at one point. I remember the first La Perouse Aboriginal community golf day at NSWGC and am really happy that this tradition has continued.[70]

Another reflection on golfing at La Perouse was provided by former Wallaby and deputy chair of the La Perouse Local Aboriginal Land Council, Lloyd Walker:

I grew up on La Perouse Aboriginal Mission down the road from the New South Wales Golf Club from the age of 10, I would wake up before the sun rose to try my hand at caddying. We would stand by a wooden fence and wait for the Golf Pro to call us up to caddy for one of the golfers. This would pay around $5-10 (in addition to a pie and a coke), which was decent pocket money for us. There were older members of the La Perouse Aboriginal community who had regulars so they would walk by the line of younger caddies and give us a nod on the way past... I still have fond memories of the time spent on New South Wales Golf Course and enjoy visiting when the opportunity arises.[71]

Like La Perouse, up at Nambucca Heads the Stuart Island Golf Club provided an avenue to raise some additional funds by caddying for golfers. The island was the former home of Aboriginal people until it was revoked as an Aboriginal reserve to make the golf course in 1955. Caddying was a way to raise money with little work around for Aboriginal people. Uncle Rob Bryant recalls

---

[70] Walker, A & Irish P (2023) *Golf on Gamay*, New South Wales Golf Club Foundation, Sydney: 26-27.

[71] Ibid.

caddying at Stuart Island Golf Club and heading to the shop to buy a bag of lollies with the money. Uncle Rob said he and his mate Kenny Moylan started acting as caddies when they were young Gumbaynggirr boys of about seven years of age. They were paid 2/6 (two shillings and sixpence) for the round and were also given a drink of lemonade at the completion of it. They would head back to Cook's Store at Bellwood and buy a bag of lollies with their cash. Uncle Rob said: 'We knew we had a start with the caddy job and supplemented that with some extra cash finding golf balls.'[72] Much respected Gumbaynggirr Elder Gary Williams is of course best remembered for attending the University of Sydney with Charles Perkins in 1964 and accompanying him on the 1965 Freedom Ride across NSW. This exposed the shocking living conditions of most Aboriginal people across the State at that time in the media.[73] In conversation with me, Gary reflected on his young life around Nambucca Heads, revealing that 'to make some money, I would act as a golf caddy and also find, collect and sell golf balls.'[74]

Both La Perouse and Stuart Island hold long histories as Aboriginal reserves. Stuart Island was originally gazetted as an Aboriginal reserve in 1883. It was taken off the community in 1955 to build the golf course. By the turn of the twentieth century, La Perouse had become a government reserve. The history of both La Perouse and Nambucca Heads is embedded in the rise of organised Aboriginal political activism in the 1920s. Prominent La Perouse Elder Jim Major was an office bearer and organiser of the Australian Aboriginal Progessive Association (AAPA) in Sydney when they formed in 1924. He was 'known to be the last full blood Aboriginal in La Perouse... He looked like a statesman with his white hair and dark skin'.[75] The AAPA infuriated the NSW Aborigines

---

[72] Interview with Uncle Rob Bryant via telephone 26 July 2022.

[73] Rolls, M & Johnson, M (2011) *Historical Dictionary of Australian Aborigines*, Scarecrow Press, Maryland: Pg.77.

[74] Conversation with Gary Williams at Nambucca Heads 23 December 1923.

[75] Nugent, M (ed.) (1988) *La Perouse – the place, the people and the sea*, Aboriginal Studies Press, Canberra: 27

Protection Board with their actions on the north coast removing Eileen Buchanan from the Protection Board's control and returning her back to her family on Stuart Island.[76]

There are many incidents of Aboriginal ingenuity in earning money in and around golf courses. Journalist Daniel Browning's grandmother Mary grew up in what is now Surfers Paradise on the Gold Coast in Queensland on one of the first land allotments ever granted on what would later become Cavill Avenue. The land was purchased by her hardworking South Sea Islander grandfather Charley Emzin. Daniel recalled that 'Nan used to scout for Jim Cavill's stray golf balls with her beloved brother Chilla'.[77] Jim Cavill was one of the major players in the development of the Gold Coast and campaigned for its name to be changed from Elston to the same name as the hotel he had built – Surfers Paradise.

Danial Browning's Grandmother Mary hunted for golf balls at Surfers Paradise.

---

[76] Maynard, J (2024) *Fight for Liberty and Freedom*, Aboriginal Studies Press, Canberra: 59.

[77] Browning, D (2023) Facebook Post, 1 June 2023.

There are also many incidents of Aboriginal people being co-opted to work as caddies. For example, an article in the *Adelaide Advertiser* in 1928 seemed to give glowing coverage of the removal of Aboriginal girls from their families' 'nomadic unstable impulses'.[78] The racist article stated that these young girls are ideal for a woman accustomed to golf as they will find the caddy an 'unwearied companion. Kindness, they repay, we are told, with a love that is almost incredible and a fidelity almost unequalled on earth'.[79] There was little understanding that these young girls had been taken from their families with little thought or understanding of the long-term psychological trauma. Many were never to return to their families and during the 1980s this child removal policy of thousands of Aboriginal children would earn the 'Stolen Generations' name.

Two Inland Mission Sisters built an outback golf course with the aid of Aboriginal helpers at Innamincka near the South Australian/Queensland border, 400 miles north of Broken Hill. Sister Gaye Manderville Halls and her sister Doreen were responsible for introducing golf to this most unlikely location. They constructed a nine-hole golf course to a location where the temperature rose to 124 degrees in the shade at the height of summer. The golf course was given the name "Dead Horse Links".[80] The most treacherous hole was the one known as the "Dead Horse Hole". The hole gained its name because a horse died alongside it after the course had been completed. 'Sometimes we didn't get past that hole, said Sister Gaye'.[81]

Some of the other holes also gained notable names, including the "The Stockyard Hole", "The Swamp Hole", "The Gibber Hole", and best of all "The Clubhouse Hole". These names give an indication of the type of country upon which the golf course was situated. The article went on to describe that golf at the course was not amateurish – Sister Gaye described that they had

---

[78] *Adelaide Advertiser,* 7 July 1928: 22

[79] Ibid.

[80] *The Herald (Melbourne),* 20 June 1936: 23

[81] Ibid.

Sister Gaye Mandeville Halls playing golf on Dead Horse Links, with 5-year-old Bossy as her Caddy.

to make special flags to mark the fairways; 'if we hadn't had them, we'd have soon lost our way'.[82] Very young Aboriginal children were used as caddies. The sisters had '5-year-old Bossy and little Mabel, two full-blooded Aborigines to caddy for them'.[83] They related that it was not too difficult to introduce golf to the outback. Sister Gaye revealed that one of the men had a set of clubs but had never used them out there. 'But he was an easy convert and within a few months golf was a minor craze'.[84] The article stated that the local Aboriginal people just looked on somewhat bemused by the spectacle. Innamincka was now known for its golf course but before the sisters' arrival, it was known only for its 'bottle heap and dust storms… the sand hills and the miles of

---

[82] Ibid.

[83] Ibid.

[84] Ibid.

gibber country relieved by stunted trees'.[85]

The *West Australian* in 1936 revealed the presence of Aboriginal caddies in the west. Captain of the Nedlands Golf Club, C. Pascoe, playing at the 'vastly improved Cottesloe links' won the visitors handicap event with a neat 81 – 10 – 71 (inward 37). He had "aced" the 170-yard third hole to the accompaniment of shrill "yackis" from his diminutive Aboriginal caddy. The news was relayed to the 80 members in the clubhouse at the time and Pascoe paid the usual penalty on his return to the club. By all accounts, the hole had been an 'adventurous one for Pascoe. Four years earlier he holed out in one and in the first round yesterday he drove nicely onto the green and then had to pursue a dog which made off into the scrub with his ball.'[86]

Aboriginal Golf Caddy Humour

Aboriginal people have a great sense of humour, and nothing gives us greater pleasure than to take the piss out of some unsuspecting whitefella. It appears our golf caddies over time were no different. Varied newspaper articles and locations across the country draw references to this caddy humour. In 1947 at the Australian-Pymble inter-club game at La Perouse, Pymble player T.G. McGee hit a shot that he lost sight of. He turned to his little Aboriginal caddy and said: "Did you see where that went, son?"

"No. It went too fast for me, boss," replied the kid.[87]

Another Aboriginal boy at the NSW course was doing his best to supplement his ball collecting. He was noted for watching the crows closely to see where they flew off to when they took off with a ball. One of their hiding places netted him three dozen balls.[88]

---

85 *The Herald (Melbourne),* 20 June 1936: 23

86 *The West Australian,* 17 July 1936: 11

87 *Daily Telegraph,* 17 August 1947: 46

88 *Daily Telegraph,* 6 July 1941: 18

Another young Aboriginal caddy was far too quick for his player. The player at La Perouse was noted as a novice: "Two Ton" Tom Moon. Having been allotted a young Aboriginal caddy, he stepped up. "Tom's first drive trickled feebly along the ground for about ten yards." The Aboriginal caddy turned to the other caddy and said, "What do you think of that?" and "He's big enough to hit it out of sight".[89]

At the NSW Golf Club, 'George Gates, Pat Rhodes, Keith Harris, and a visitor played in a four-ball. On the last green, the visitor took three putts. He swished his club with annoyance and said disgustedly, "Another one. I'd like to know how many greens I've done that on today." His small Aboriginal caddy, who had not said a word during the round. interjected with:"Seventeen."[90]

An important historical fact is that in the far north of the country in Darwin, Aboriginal inmates from Fanny Bay gaol had originally been co-opted to help construct the Darwin golf course.[91] Golfers who were taking part in the 1953 Darwin Golf Club's annual tournament had been disturbed by the discovery of wild buffalo tracks on the first fairway. Following the discovery, a few of the members had trouble keeping their heads down. They kept glancing about for a potentially stampeding wild buffalo. It was noted that an Aboriginal caddy named Jimmy, who was 'caddying for the club captain, T. D. Harris, saw the

A youthful golf enthusiast

---

[89] *Daily Telegraph*, 25 March, 1939

[90] *Daily Telegraph*, 20 July 1947: 44

[91] Ibid.

tracks first. Jimmy, who rarely speaks during a round, suddenly became excited. Pointing to the tracks, he shouted, "Him buffalo!" It was noted that 'Jimmy, who comes from Milingimbi, knows his buffalo'.[92]

Apparently, the club already had local rules to 'provide for lifting the ball from kangaroo scrape or a hole made by sea crabs which burrow on the course. The Committee is now considering an amendment to include a plan if a buffalo appears. They will run.' This wasn't the only hazard. One fairway 'borders a mangrove swamp from which thousands of crabs crawl at night and burrow holes in the turf'. It was noted that hawks and kites are ever in the sky on the lookout for golf balls. Over twenty years before, the Darwin course had been described in the following terms: 'fairways on the Darwin course run through the jungle, and many greens are surrounded by pandanus palms. Sweet roots are plentiful, and in the early mornings, wallabies and bandicoots scratch up the fairways to get at them.'[93]

An article drew attention to the fact that there was an endeavour to prevent boys stealing the golf balls on the St Michael's course at La Perouse. It was decided there would be an organised drive to round up the culprits. 'A cordon was formed round the course and netted several boys. Among them an Aboriginal boy. They were all marched into the office of a very stern, police-looking committee man sitting behind a table. He barked out a warning to all to frighten the daylights out of the boys. "This sort of thing will have to stop. I'll have to make examples of you. What's your name?" he bawled at the Aboriginal boy. "Jack Johnson" was the prompt reply. Obviously named in honour of African American boxing champion Jack Johnson, a great hero of the Aboriginal community. The committee man next looked at a little white youngster standing next to the Aboriginal boy. "What's yours?" he bellowed at the boy. "He's my brother" said the Aboriginal kid and shattered the solemnity of the proceedings'.[94]

In 1953, a newspaper report highlighted the skill, talent and expertise of an

---

92 *Kalgoorlie Miner,* 5 August 1953: 8

93 *World's News (Sydney),* 4 September 1935: 13

94 *Daily Telegraph,* 8 June 1941: 25

Aboriginal caddy. It highlighted that an Aboriginal caddy simply named Gus played a central role in helping Bill Gluth and Bill Edgar win the Australian Foursomes Championship in Sydney. It was reported that Gus had been caddying for Gluth ever since the Victorian had arrived in Sydney. Gus left the course at La Perouse on Monday evening after play had finished and had been under the impression that the foursome's play-off would not take place until the following Sunday. But traveling on a tram in Sydney early on Tuesday morning looking over someone's shoulder at the newspaper, Gus saw that Gluth and Edgar were playing that very morning. He 'immediately jumped off the tram, caught a taxi and arrived at the course just as Gluth and Edgar were hitting off.'[95] Gluth remarked after the victory, 'It was wonderful to see Gus running up to us. He's the best caddy I've ever had, and I knew we'd win the tournament the moment I saw him coming.'[96]

Former top Aboriginal boxer Billy Samuels, who had some great fights at the Sydney Stadium during the 1920s, also had some humorous insight to the game of golf. Samuels was noted as saying that he had been reading in the newspapers 'that some of my countrymen have taken on golf', adding that boxers like 'Gene Tunney and Jack Dempsey all play golf'. Billy was adamant that he saw no reason 'why I shouldn't give the game a fly'.

I can run, fight, ride a horse, so I don't see why I can't play golf too. There's plenty of golf paddocks round these country towns. I've just been thinking that if I learn a few uppercuts with that there niblick, a man oughta be able to get a bet on with some of them bush novices. I won't take on any champions for a month or two but there's plenty of fellas in the bush that fancy themselves at anything from fighting to playing golf. I'll get Bob Yow Yeh, the South Sea Islander to caddy for me. That wild fella will scare the wits out of my opponents. Me and Bob would make a good combination and when I teach him the game,

---

95 *Daily News (Perth)*, 23 September 1953: 17

96 Ibid.

he can go back to the South Sea Islands and fetch his mates. I believe in international sport.[97]

A report in the Sydney press highlighted that a Queensland station owner was a very keen golfer. He practised on a rough links course he had constructed in a paddock on his property. One day, he requisitioned a young Aboriginal girl, whom he had found prowling around the store, to be his caddy. By all accounts, it was not one of his better days in hitting golf balls:

and as his play drifted from bad to worse his language proportionately grew more lurid. He did not expect his Australian language to be understood by the girl. At the seventh hole he ricked his back, and the air became blue.

Miss "Black" turned on him then. "Excuse me. Sir" she said, "but your language is unbecoming. I'll have you understand that I'll not tolerate it from anyone." It transpired later that she was from a mission settlement and was well educated.[98]

Historically, golf did present some opportunities to earn some income from caddying for Aboriginal people, but it all depended on location, proximity and access to a golf course. But the history of Aboriginal people across the nineteenth and greater part of the twentieth century is one of severe and strict control over their lives and opportunities.

---

[97] *Sporting Globe (Melbourne)*, 12 October 1927: 10

[98] *Sydney Mail*, 2 July 1930: 57

The Golf Course Burial Sites – Skeletons in the Bunker

This chapter, focusing on the proliferation of Aboriginal burial sites on golf courses across the country, is also a reflection on the burial and erasure of Aboriginal history and memory from so many golf locations. Anthropologist W.E.H. Stanner defined this Australian history as the 'Great Australian Silence' in the 1968 ABC Boyer Lecture.[99] He was pointing to the fact that Australian history had all but erased an Aboriginal historical presence. This silence has also been reflected on many golf courses across the country.

Golf writer Peter Owen has highlighted the beauty and splendour of the water-surrounded golf course at Nambucca Heads, the Stuart Island golf course occupying its own '35 ha island near where the Nambucca River empties into the Pacific Ocean'.[100] It is, in Owen's words, a 'tight, but picturesque and immensely playable course that is surrounded by water, on every side, providing spectacular views and a sense of calm and beauty.'[101] I have played the course a number of times over the years and can attest to its quality and the beauty of the location. As to the background and history of the location, Owen revealed that the island 'was used to mill timber that had been floated downriver – and curiously, to train greyhounds – until a nine-hole golf course was established not long after the end of World War 2'.[102] Owen did not

---

99   Stanner, W.E.H (1991) *After the Dreaming*, ABC Books, Sydney: Pg. 18.

100 Owen, P (2022) Play Golf Surrounded by Water, *Inside Golf*, August 2022, pp: 42-43.

101 Ibid: 42

102 Peter Owen, 2022 Play Golf Surrounded by Water, *Inside Golf*, August 2022, pp: 42-43.

Gary Williams and Charlie Perkins at the University of Sydney 1964.

mention the true and long history of the site and its connection to the local Aboriginal Gumbaynggirr people.

Stuart Island was a very significant cultural location for the local Gumbaynggirr people. Known as Girriigirr, it was originally gazetted to the local people as a reserve in 1883. That year saw the establishment of the New South Wales government's Aborigines Protection Board, and the island was given to the local Aboriginal people in its first year of operation. They would retain Stuart Island as their home until 1955 when they were forced off – to make way for the golf course.

Gumbaynggirr Elder Gary Williams recalled that his 'mum was moved off the Aboriginal reserve at Stuart Island to make way for the golf course. Later she would be moved off the reserve at Bowraville to make way for another golf course to be made. The community at Moree were also moved to make way for a golf course.'[103]

Aboriginal people have suffered in the wake of the 1983 NSW Aboriginal Land Rights Act and the Mabo and native title decisions during the 1990s.

---

[103] Conversation with Gary Williams at Nambucca Heads 23 December 1923.

Many in the wider community, including golf clubs and their members, were stampeded with hysteria that Aboriginal people were going to somehow take control of the Sydney Opera House, their backyard dunny and their prized golf clubs. The stupidity and ignorance of such nonsense and the complete lack of any understanding of the miniscule amount of Aboriginal people who could regain land was responsible for unleashing a terrible backlash of racial resentment.

Following the 1983 Aboriginal Land Rights Act in NSW, a newspaper headline in Nambucca Heads read 'Aborigines will never get the island'. The State Member for Coffs Harbour, Mr Matt Singleton, had bluntly asserted at a specially convened meeting of the National Party that 'legislation recently passed by State Parliament made it impossible for Aborigines to win any court case'[104] and 'Aborigines would never get control of Stuart Island'.[105] When passing land rights legislation just before Easter, the NSW parliament had also eliminated any illegality that might have occurred when land, such as Stuart Island, was transferred from the Aboriginal Lands Board.[106] It was explained that there had been 'some doubt about the legality of the transfer, but the Bill had removed that doubt, Mr Singleton said'.[107] Going further, Singleton asserted: 'The law of the land states that these acquisitions were valid.'[108] At the meeting, a Dr Tom Fennell raised the question: 'That's a bit tough on the Aborigines.' Mr Singleton blurted with authority: 'We are one nation. And Aborigines can play golf on Stuart Island just as anyone else can.'[109]

This heated debate had been in the local press for several months and been a discussion topic within the local council. One member of the town council, Councillor Ledger, alleged in the media that local Aboriginal people

---

104 *Nambucca Guardian News*, 22 April 1983: 1

105 Ibid.

106 *Nambucca Guardian News*, 22 April 1983: 1

107 Ibid.

108 Ibid.

109 Ibid.

had mounted a land grab on the golf course 'on the quiet'. Some very prominent members of the Nambucca Aboriginal community responded with a well-crafted argument in the letters to the editor section of the *Nambucca Guardian News:*

Cr Ledger's allegation of a 'quiet land grab' by Aboriginal people could be better directed at the Nambucca Heads Island Golf Club. The club's advertisements, in the form of a petition, printed in the *Guardian News,* admits that the club occupied the island for seven years (1948-55), while it was still an Aboriginal reserve. The Aboriginal people of the Nambucca were never consulted on the 'quiet land grab'. Rather than us doing things on the quiet, in 1978 via press releases to the *Sydney Morning Herald,* we made it plain that we were lodging a land claim. The golf club nonetheless went ahead and sought to entrench itself. They did this by converting the special lease which applied to that land around the clubhouse to freehold title. In other words, in 1980 the club managed to alienate this particular piece of Crown Land. None of the Aboriginal claimants were consulted – a further quiet land grab. We wonder if CR Hicks and Ledger would care to publicly state their position on this method of quiet conversion of leases whereby Crown Land becomes private land.[110]

The Aboriginal responders pointed out that a similar procedure was underway regarding access to the Nambucca River foreshore areas. They demanded to know what role the council was playing in this process and were of the opinion that local residents were not being consulted and 'whether their interests are being met'.[111] The Aboriginal writers were adamant that the signatories to a petition mounted by the golf club were 'unwittingly playing a

---

[110] *Nambucca Guardian News,* 16 July 1982: 5

[111] *Nambucca Guardian News,* 16 July 1982: 5

supportive role in the continuing takeover of Aboriginal lands'.[112] Councillor Ledger, wanting to discredit, undermine and deride the local Aboriginal community, had targeted the Aboriginal community at Bellwood in the press. The Aboriginal letter delivered a powerful and cutting response:

> If Councillor Ledger also thinks Bellwood is a "shocking disgrace", and thinks it should be improved, he should explain why several years ago, Department of Aboriginal Affairs' funds were used by council to employ Aboriginal people – not to improve the reserve – but ironically, to make improvements to the golf course! The shoring up of the southern portion of the island was done with Aboriginal labour and Aboriginal Affairs' funds![113]

The letter highlighted the fact that the Aboriginal community were open to discussion on the land claim and had made that clear to the public and were very critical of the 'siege mentality' of Councillors Ledger and Hicks. The letter to the editor was signed by very prominent Aboriginal Elders and community members: Rita Whaddy Bryant, Vilma Whaddy Moylan, Josephine Mary Bryant Munro, Gary Williams and Jessie Williams.[114] Despite the controversy and conflict over Stuart Island, eventually a special sign was erected at the request of the Aboriginal community to highlight the presence of an Aboriginal burial site on the island.

Instead of the 'siege mentality', golf clubs like Stuart Island and many others would be far better off promoting their connection to Aboriginal people and culture and developing strong, close relationships with their local Aboriginal communities. These partnerships can only help promote their courses. Why not a sign coming onto a golf course acknowledging the fact that this is the traditional land of the local Aboriginal people for instance, in the case of

---

112 Ibid.

113 Ibid.

114 Ibid.

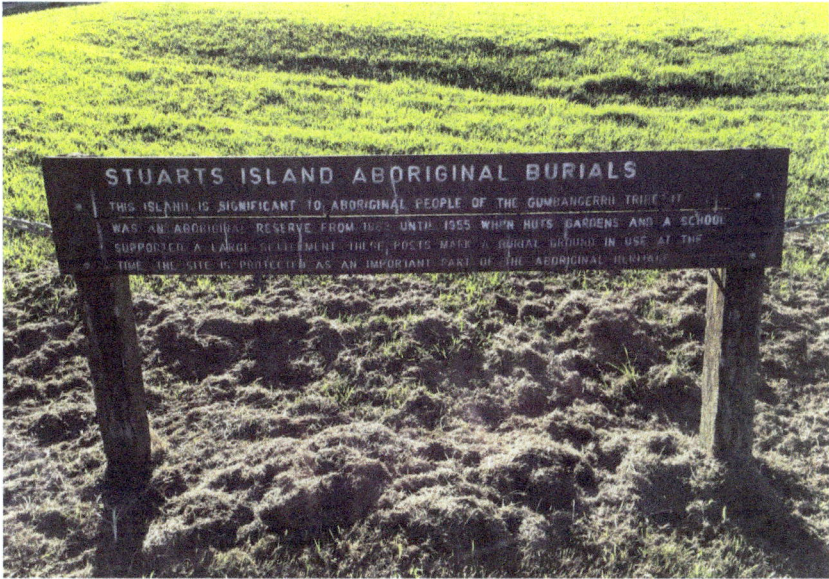

The Burial Site marker on Stuart's Island Golf Course.

Newcastle Golf Club, the 'Worimi' people. Why not fly the Aboriginal flag and display some Aboriginal artwork? Look to employ some young Aboriginal greenkeepers and encourage young Aboriginal golfers into the game?

There are numerous historical accounts of bad behaviour surrounding golf clubs and Aboriginal culture and people. A report in 1989 saw Aboriginal people 'seeking the preservation and protection from further injury of a number of significant Aboriginal areas located on the Murray Downs Golf and Country Club in New South Wales near Swan Hill' under the *Aboriginal and Torres Strait islander Heritage and Protection Act.* It was indicated that a map had been provided showing the locations of the areas and that further information could be obtained from the Department of Aboriginal Affairs.[115]

In 1993 in the Australian Capital Territory, a developer violated an Aboriginal site. The ACT government denounced 'the violation of an Aboriginal heritage

---

[115] Commonwealth of Australia Gazette. Special (national: 1977 -2012), Friday 28 April 1989 (NO. S147), page 1.

site in the construction of the Gungahlin Golf Course Estate'.[116] It was noted that the site concerned was 'an old quarry used jointly by Aborigines and European settlers to obtain chert' and that a specific course of action could include a $5,000 fine or ultimately the withdrawal of the lease.[117]

Clearly these were not just isolated incidents, and as recently as 2013, Tasmanian Aboriginal people were angered by the wanton destruction of thousands of mutton bird nests on King Island to make way for the construction of a new golf course. Aboriginal Land Council spokesman Clyde Mansell said the development should be halted before any more burrows were destroyed. It was estimated that some 12,000 burrows had been bulldozed during the construction of the golf course. Birds fly from the Northern Hemisphere on their annual migration. Muttonbirding has been a longstanding Tasmanian Aboriginal food harvesting tradition. Mansell demanded that 'the developer should be brought to pay for the damage that has occurred there'.[118] The development spokesman, Darius Oliver, defended the project, stating 'that only 6,000 nests had been destroyed'.[119] He called the Aboriginal response 'a little bit alarmist'.[120]

The State government defended the developer's approval stating that 'the developer has had to meet several conditions and work has been done to minimise potential impacts on birds'.[121] Eric Woehler of Birds Tasmania was highly critical stating that 'the golf course was approved without a proper scientific assessment'.[122] He went on to clarify: 'These birds are going to be trying to nest in the area that the colonies used to occupy and by destroying the colonies these birds are going to be fighting for whatever burrowing

---

[116] *Canberra Times*, 26 January 1993: 3

[117] Ibid.

[118] *ABC News*, 27 September 2013.

[119] Ibid.

[120] Ibid.

[121] Ibid.

[122] Ibid.

habitat is available to them. It's going to have an impact on the population.'[123]

What are now recognised to be two world-class golf courses – Cape Wickham and Ocean Dunes – were opened in 2015 and 2016 respectively. But in this 21st century of global warming, rising temperatures, rising sea levels, catastrophic storms, floods and fires, people will eventually need to wake up and consider the full impact of their actions.

There are so many golf clubs around the country that are completely unaware of sites of great Aboriginal significance, including burial sites, on their courses. It was recorded in Stockton that many 'Aboriginal skeletons had been unearthed in various parts of the district in similar circumstances in recent years.'[124] As an example, back in 1900 an Aboriginal skeleton had been unearthed on Stockton Beach by Senior Constable M'Kellar. The spot where the remains were found is believed to have once been an Aboriginal burying place, as other portions of other human skeletons have been washed up at different times.'[125] Similarly, in 1949 a Mr James Bryant of Stockton found two skeletons a few hundred yards back from the beach. It was noted that only some months back, some other skeletons were unearthed near the new discovery. Experts proved the earlier remains were Aborigines from 'a native burial ground in the locality'.[126]

In 1903, a golfer playing on the course at Glenelg in South Australia 'discovered a human skeleton, which had been exposed owing to the actions of the weather. The locality was at one time an Aboriginal burial ground, and in all probability, the remains belonged to a blackfellow.'[127] The police were contacted, and on disinterring the remains, found more human bones that 'had all the appearance of having been in the ground before the advent of the white man in South Australia. I have collected many such records of Aboriginal burial

---

123 Ibid.

124 *Armidale Express and New England General Advertiser,* 4 June 1937: 3

125 *Maitland Daily Mercury,* 1 December 1900: 4

126 *Newcastle Morning Herald,* 10 October 1949: 1

127 *Evening Journal* (Adelaide) 1903: 1

Bungaree and Ricketty Dick

sites being discovered on golf courses over many decades, and these remain important cultural heritage markers today.

Some believe that Bungaree, the first known Aboriginal man to circumnavigate Australia, was buried on the site of Royal Sydney Golf Club at Rose Bay.[128] Another famous Aboriginal man who may be buried on the course was known as "Ricketty Dick" (and Warrah Warrah). He was a well-known and liked Aboriginal man between the early to mid-nineteenth century. He is known to have set up camp at Rose Bay. In 1910, the site of his 'Gunyah' was recorded as being 'about where the golf links are now'.[129] He had died in 1863, and a coin with his profile was struck after his death.

In 1905, the *Sydney Mail* reported that a nine-hole golf course had been built in western New South Wales at Wilcannia. The first tee was located 'on the western bank of the Darling River, the opposite bank being about 40 ft higher, so that to clear the latter, the drive must have a carry of at least 80 yards. To the beginner, hypnotised as so many golfers are by a water hazard close at

---

[128]   *Sydney Morning Herald,* 4 July 2020

[129]   https://ia.anu.edu.au/biography/dick-ricketty-18144

hand, this carry is awesome.'[130] The article went on to highlight the seventh hole with an excellent bunker 'situated 60 yards from the tee, and spreads about 60 yards towards the hole. Its surface is varied by certain small elevations, which the old residents declare form the graves of Aboriginals long since passed away. As may be supposed, there are many curious onlookers in the far west who marvel at what they term the "idiotic" enthusiasm of the golfer'.[131] It was declared that the way the game is being taken up there is 'a good future for golf in the Wilcannia district'.[132]

In 1920, one William Flynn, while excavating for a new building at the Royal Sydney Golf Club at Rose Bay, made a discovery 'on the site of the clubhouse, which was recently destroyed by fire, when he unearthed the skull and bones of a human, 6 feet below the surface. The remains were examined by the Government medical officer, who has reported that they are the remains of an Aboriginal buried approximately 100 years ago.'[133]

A human skull was unearthed in Adelaide on the Lockley's Golf Course in 1923. 'During the progress of the first round of the country championship at the Kooyonga course, Mr H. L. Rymill, the captain of the Kooyonga club, discovered a human skull, which is believed to be that of an Aboriginal. A number of interstate visitors were much interested in the find.'[134]

In 1937, with the construction and expansion of the Newcastle golf course at Stockton to an 18-hole course: 'two skeletons in a state of good preservation and believed to be those of an Aboriginal woman and Aboriginal girl, were found while excavations were being carried out'. The discovery at the back of the fourth green of 'the first skeleton by a party of workers who are extending the course was accompanied by considerable excitement. A cursory examination made by the party before the police were communicated with disclosed a hole

[130] *Sydney Mail and New South Wales Advertiser,* 13 September 1905: 6

[131] Ibid.

[132] Ibid.

[133] *Daily Telegraph (Sydney),* 29 November 1920: 6; *Singleton Argus,* 30 November 1920: 2

[134] *Barrier Miner (Broken Hill),* 18 August 1923: 8

The 4th green looking to the 7th tee today, where Aboriginal woman and child skeletons were unearthed in 1937. It is the highest point on the course and a large hill of sand. Aboriginal people chose sand for burial locations as digging and preserving remains was easy.

in the skull, apparently inflicted with a sharp instrument. Detective A. W. Burns and other police who went to the links concluded that the hole had been caused by a blow from one of the men's picks. The police lifted the skeleton out of the ground and in doing so found the second lying beside it. Several factors pointed to the bones being those of an Aboriginal woman and a girl, aged about 12, whose bodies had been buried together.'[135] The police stated that the skeleton was a very old one, and thought it might be that of an Aboriginal. They had no record of anyone missing from Stockton district within the last five years.

Medical officers were asked by the police to examine the skeletons. The conclusions drawn from the medical examination 'estimated that the skeletons

---

[135] *Daily Examiner (Grafton),* 7 June 1937: 4

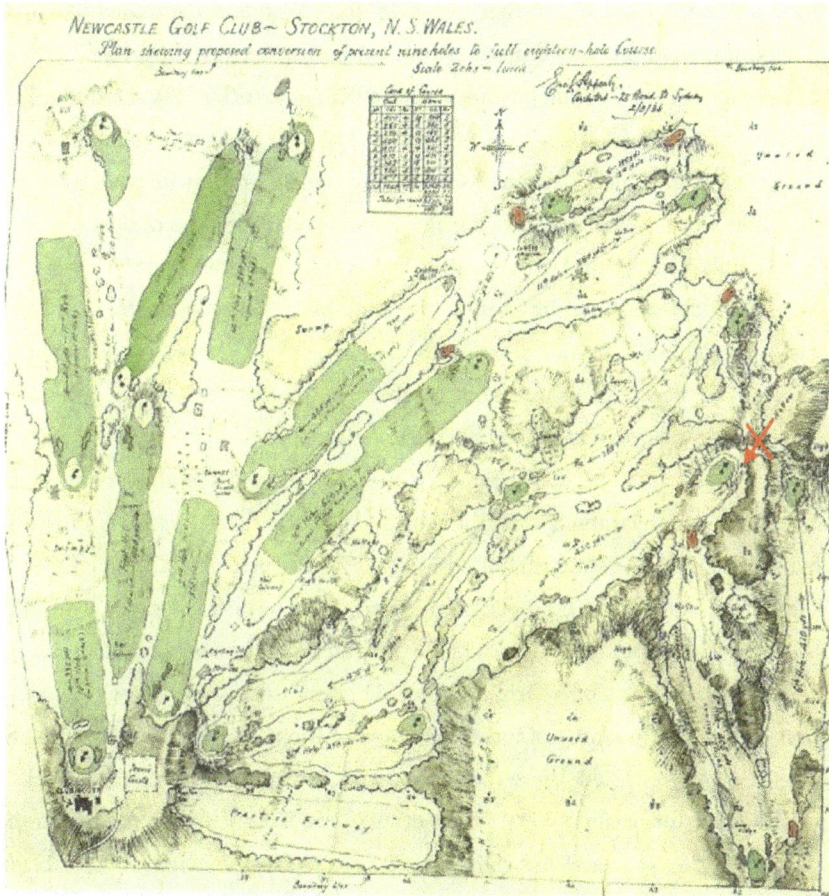

The map shows the proposed changes to the Newcastle Golf Club in 1936. The X marks the spot at the back of the 4th hole and the site of the 7th tee of the Aboriginal burial site.

had been there between 60 to 70 years. The sandy soil in which they were found had no doubt contributed to their good state of preservation.'[136] That would place the timing of the burials roughly back between the 1860s and 1870s. It is important to consider that the dates for the interment of the Aboriginal remains

---

[136] *Newcastle Sun*, 4 June 1937: 5

could stretch back much further to the 1840s – a time of continued violence being inflicted on the Worimi population.

It was left to the acting government medical officer (Dr F. W. D. Collier) to deliver his overall findings 'that one of the skulls was that of a young woman. The other skull, which was much smaller and not so strongly formed, was that of a child who had not reached the age of puberty at the time of death. In the case of children, it is hard to determine the sex from the skull alone.'[137] The other medical officer said that the skull of the 'adult bore marked sutures. These, he said, were generally an indication of Aboriginal descent.'[138] It was noted that the discovery of the skeletons was made by 'three young men – Messrs E. Jones and A. Dives of Stockton and D. Cox of Fullerton Cove'.[139]

In Victoria in 1949, it was reported that a 'skull and the almost complete skeleton of a man larger in build than the average Australian has been dug from a sandpit at the Riverside golf links, Mildura by the course caretaker, Mr J. Giles. The bones, believed to be those of an Aborigine, are possibly more than 200 years old. The upper teeth in the skull were practically undamaged.'[140]

In all these cases of Aboriginal remains being uncovered on golf courses, there is nothing recorded of what happened to the remains. It is very unlikely that they were reburied. Were they handed over to a museum or placed with a private collector or simply just disposed of? One is left to raise the question: why are there so many Aboriginal burial sites on golf courses? One clear answer is that Aboriginal people chose burial sites in soft soil, particularly sand, and they are often in or near Aboriginal middens and places of occupation.[141] The disturbing thing about many of these historical accounts of Aboriginal remains being uncovered on golf courses are that they are so blasé and dismissive. There is an utter disregard, disrespect and ignorance of the fact

---

[137] *Newcastle Sun*, 4 June 1937: 5

[138] Ibid.

[139] Ibid.

[140] *Argus (Melbourne)*, 18 November 1949: 5

[141] https://www.firstpeoplesrelations.vic.gov.au/fact-sheet-aboriginal-burials

that these are burial sites. Aboriginal people regard burial sites with great significance, and they are locations of deep spiritual emotion. One only has to compare when a non-Indigenous cemetery is damaged or destroyed by vandals. There is an immediate hue and cry in the media over the destruction. Aboriginal burial sites need the same reverence and protection.

It was noted in the *Sydney Morning Herald* in 2020 that 'repeated discoveries of Aboriginal remains and stone artefacts in sand dunes at Rose Bay's Royal Sydney Golf Club have prompted archaeologists to warn that its proposed $17 million redevelopment may lead to more finds.'[142] The archaeologists involved in undertaking the study 'have applied to register the 43-hectare championship course as an area of cultural sensitivity, as a precautionary measure'. This will allow test excavations to 'identify whether further remains and artefacts exist on the site before construction begins in 2021'.[143]

Chief executive officer of the La Perouse local Aboriginal Land Council, Chris Ingrey, 'backed the need for explorative works before construction begins'.[144] Ingrey was very appreciative of the Royal Sydney Golf Club, saying that their 'respect and treatment of culturally sensitive remains was a model to other organisations. They are very appreciative of Aboriginal heritage, and they understand the significance.'[145] He noted that the club had commissioned research and exploratory work before starting construction, while other owners dig first.

What a welcome change to the bad old days of the past, including the hysteria of the 1970s to 1990s when the policy was to destroy and block any evidence of Aboriginal connection. Historian and archaeologist Paul Irish commented that the Rose Bay area was known as Pannerong and the 'landscape was not just a larder. It was rich in meaning for Aboriginal people.'[146]

---

142 *Sydney Morning Herald,* 4 July 2020

143 Ibid.

144 Ibid.

145 Ibid.

146 Ibid.

Things are slowly changing and farsighted clubs like New South Wales Golf Club are recognising the changing times. Through greater knowledge and understanding, they have produced a wonderful booklet written by Ash Walker and Paul Irish – *Golf on Gamay* – that celebrates their course and its long connection to local Aboriginal people and culture. This is exactly the policy and practice that needs to be encouraged around the country.

Aboriginal Golfers and Reflections

It was not until the 1970s that we witnessed a steady rise of Aboriginal people playing and enjoying golf. This chapter will highlight some who have played the game with varying levels of success. They remain as a source of inspiration for future generations of Aboriginal players.

The 1960s heralded a time of great social and political change. There was an enormously divisive war in Vietnam and the civil rights movement in the United States led by Dr Martin Luther King generated worldwide attention to the plight and inequality of African American life in the United States. It was also a time of great change in Australia, and Aboriginal people suddenly appeared from the shadows and neglect of Australia's past. Charles Perkins and a group of students from the University of Sydney emulated the 'Freedom Rides' of the civil rights movement in the United States. In 1965, Perkins and the students took a bus across New South Wales exposing the shocking living conditions of Aboriginal people and the severe segregation that impacted Aboriginal life.

In 1966, the Gurindji people walked off Wave Hill Station and demanded better conditions and pay for their work as stockmen and women. They eventually demanded the return of their traditional lands. In the 1967 Federal referendum, nearly 91% of the Australian community supported Aboriginal people being counted in the census and the Commonwealth government taking charge of Aboriginal affairs. The protest period culminated with the establishment of the Aboriginal Tent Embassy in 1972 on the lawns of Parliament House in Canberra. The Embassy generated international media attention to the Aboriginal fight for rights and justice in Australia.

During this period, we also witnessed Aboriginal people breaking free of sporting exclusion. World bantamweight boxing champion Lionel Rose, tennis Grand Slam tournament winner Evonne Goolagong and champion jockey Darby McCarthy were just a few who gained international sporting recognition. Both rugby league and Australian football saw an incredible rise in Aboriginal participation from the 1970s onwards, breaking through the previous colour barriers of exclusion. Aboriginal Australia has produced some of Australia's greatest sporting talent, and despite limited opportunities, golf has also produced some top Aboriginal players at various levels. Golf was slow to match other sports with Aboriginal player participation. Of course, the cost of golf equipment and gaining access to golf courses remained the major barriers.

There are some rare examples of Aboriginal players prior to the 1960s. As far back as 1958, Aboriginal talent was being observed where opportunity was given. In the schoolboy golf championship held at Concord that year where Canberra student Gerald Focken won the title, Colin Faulkner from Kempsey – 'the only full-blooded Aborigine to ever take part in a golf championship' – finished third, only two shots behind the winner with scores of 84-81.[147] Harold Blair, the celebrated Aboriginal tenor, was noted as having sporting interests. He played cricket, squash and tennis on the weekends. He also practised weightlifting and physical culture and had 'recently taken up golf'.[148]

Scott Gardiner – US PGA Golfer

Scott Gardiner is unquestionably the highest-achieving Aboriginal golfer the game has seen. Gardiner took Aboriginal golf into another stratosphere when he qualified for the United States PGA Tour. Tiger Woods unknowingly was the inspiration for Gardiner's golfing career. Gardiner was part of a program that was started in the late 1990s by ex-rugby league player David Liddiard and run

---

[147] *Biz (Fairfield)*, 21 May 1958: Pg. 6.

[148] *Queensland Times*, 21 December 1946: Pg. 7; *Coolgardie Miner (WA)*, 2 June 1949, Pg.3.

through the National Aboriginal Sports Corporation called "Hunt for the Australian Tiger".[149] Coming through that program and going on to earn his United States PGA Tour card saw Gardiner excited and adamant that he wanted to inspire other young Aboriginal golfers: 'I am very proud... it's a great feeling,' he said. 'Hopefully I can help inspire a few others to go for a career in golf and I hope I can be a role model.'[150]

Gardiner had finally made the big promotion to the PGA Tour at the age of 36 in 2012, after several near misses in 2007 and 2009. 'There is certainly some relief. Until you get there you never really know if you're ever going to make it... But now I am there and it's a big thrill for me and my parents who are over here this week and who always supported my dreams.'[151]

Gardiner (recorded as the oldest rookie on the PGA Tour) had an Aboriginal mother and Scottish father. An article in the *New York Times* explained that he was the product of a working-class Sydney suburb and a program 'created to identify and develop the Australian Tiger Woods.'[152] He was excited to be playing at Torrey Pines in a tournament where Tiger Woods was the 36-hole leader. 'It's pretty neat to be standing here at Torrey Pines, at a tournament that I've watched numerous years, and really finding out how good Tiger is, shooting 11 under.'[153] Gardiner made the weekend cut at 1 under and was content. 'I played about as good as I can play, and he's 10 shots better.'[154]

As a child, Gardiner played soccer but switched to golf after he was invited to join the National Aboriginal Sports Corporation's golf development program. He is the program's most successful product and has developed a high profile because of his Aboriginal background. In his first year on the PGA Tour in 2013, 'He began the season at the Sony Open in Hawaii being shadowed by a

---

[149] *Sydney Morning Herald,* 4 December 2012

[150] *Sydney Morning Herald,* 30 October 2012

[151] *Herald Sun,* 29 October 2012

[152] *New York Times,* 26 January 2013

[153] Ibid.

[154] Ibid.

Scott Gardiner tees off.

documentary filmmaker for a 30-minute short. He finished tied for 15th.'[155]

Gardiner had turned pro in 2000 and made 199 starts over 10 years on the lower-level, developmental PGA Tour, earning US$1.6 million. It was enough to pay his bills. And here he was, competing against Tiger Woods at the highest level in the game.[156] Gardiner was something of a golfing prodigy after coming through the 'amateur ranks in 1993; that year he was a member of the NSW and Australian junior teams and was a NSW schoolboy champion. He finished eleventh in the 1999 Australian Open.'[157] He went on to play on the European Tour before heading to the United States. In 2014, Gardiner highlighted the highs and lows of life as a pro golfer:

> Pretty tough… I quite enjoy the travel; the places I've been through golf
> I couldn't have gone through any other occupation. But I've got a 6-year-

---

[155] *New York Times*, 26 January 2013

[156] Ibid.

[157] Tatz, C & Tatz, P (2018) *Black Pearls – The Aboriginal and islander Sports Hall of Fame*, Aboriginal Studies Press, Canberra: 23

old boy, and a 14-year-old girl and they miss their dad a lot. I like to be at their events and also to lessen the workload for my wife, who's doing a two- person job on her own.[158]

There were some perks for a golfing family as the 'tournaments try to outdo each other when hosting players.' Gardiner highlighted:

At one tournament they opened up Sea World just for the PGA players and their families. At the Arnold Palmer Invitational at Bay Hill, Florida, we all got to go to Walt Disney World.[159]

Gardiner has some cherished memories from the Tour including a pairing with Phil Mickelson at the Wells Fargo Championship. It can be clearly intimidating at times:

Playing with Phil at the Wells Fargo Championship was the most people I've ever seen on the first tee. I had to take a moment to gather myself, but with so much adrenalin I stepped up and hit it 300m off the tee, overshot my wedge in but then chipped in. It was an amazing feeling.[160]

Gardiner stated that his best finish on tour was a tie for 13th at the Pebble Beach National Pro- Am, and that it was a very special moment. 'My dad was there, and it was cool for him to be at such an iconic course, walking among celebrities like Clint Eastwood.'[161]

There was also the opportunity to forge a strong friendship with fellow

---

[158] https://www.foxsports.com.au/golf/scott-gardiner-chipping-away-as-an-aussie-nomad-golfer-with-his-family-half-the-world-away/news-story/416b99f579357d54afdf72326d437546

[159] Ibid.

[160] https://www.foxsports.com.au/golf/scott-gardiner-chipping-away-as-an-aussie-nomad-golfer-with-his-family-half-the-world-away/news-story/416b99f579357d54afdf72326d437546

[161] Ibid.

Aboriginal sports star, basketballer Patty Mills. It provided Gardiner with the opportunity to hang out in the San Antonio Spurs' dressing room. Mills reciprocated and was 'spotted cheering on Gardiner from the PGA Tour galleries – in such outfits as a Queensland Maroons' State of Origin Jersey and an Australian tracksuit.'[162] Gardiner stated that he and Mills were 'both of Indigenous Australian heritage, so there was a connection. I've had the pleasure of getting to know him; he's a great bloke. I've been to a few of his games, and he watches me at golf tournaments whenever he can.'

A golf career at the top can be a roller coaster experience. In 2014, Gardiner teed up at the Australian Golf Club in the Australian Open in Sydney. After opening with a double bogey, Gardiner 'redeemed himself with the shot of the day on the 11th hole, sinking a hole in one'.[163] That shot won him a brand new Lexus NX car. Jordan Spieth won the event with a score of 13 under par.

Soon afterwards, Scott Gardiner was ravaged by injuries that basically cost him two years out of the game. He lost his US Tour Card and in 2016 was on the comeback trail trying to earn his place back at the top level in the Web.com Tour.[164] Sadly, Gardiner did not achieve his goal but in any estimation remains an inspiring figure for any young Aboriginal golfer.

Today, he operates Scott Gardiner Golf Instruction online and teaches golf at *Paradise Valley Athletic Club in Fayetteville, Arkansas.* At the same time as Scott Gardiner emerged, there were two other Aboriginal golf professionals – Wayne Smith from Perth, who finished tenth in the Australian Order of Merit in 1999-2000, and Nicole Kowien from Queensland.

Mark Chalker

Mark Chalker did not start playing golf until he was sixteen, but he was quickly smitten with the game. He started as a trainee professional at Hillview Public

---

[162] Ibid.

[163] *Sydney Morning Herald,* 27 November 2014;

[164] https://pga.org.au/news/gardiner-trying-to-build-on-good-start/

Golf Course in Perth. In 1979, Mark joined his mother May to win the Western Australian Mixed Foursomes. Eventually, he was taken on as an assistant professional at Huntingdale in Melbourne. This was significant in that he was recognised as the first Aboriginal to 'appear in Australian professional golf'.[165] At the time, he was noted as being committed to the game and wanting to make a name for himself in the professional ranks. Mark eventually found his way back to the west and has been at Hillview delivering specialised coaching golf lessons with over thirty years' experience.

Brad Hardman

There are lessons at all levels of the game for young Aboriginal kids coming through about overcoming setbacks and making the right life choices. None are more powerful than those of boxing trainer Brad Hardman. Brad made one of those wrong choices at the age of fifteen when a friend grabbed the keys to his parents' car, and he joined a group of mates to take it for a joy ride. There were no substances in use, but none of the kids had a licence. The car crashed after it hit a telegraph pole. The speedometer was frozen on impact, and they were traveling at least 120 kilometres per hour. The car was ripped in two. Brad ended up in the trunk with a leg 'severed and my pelvis was broken in several spots'.[166] Brad's friend Robbie was killed in the accident. Brad spent months in hospital:

doing rehab and learning to walk with a prosthesis. I'll spare you the details. What was most horrible was knowing I'd never play sport again. I boxed a lot, but ever since the age of 4, my dream had been to play rugby league. Some of the guys I played with as a kid went on to compete for New South Wales and Australia.[167]

---

[165] Pollard, J (1990) *Australian Golf,* Angus & Robertson, Sydney: pg.1-2.

[166] *Golf Digest,* 16 December 2010

[167] Ibid.

But there was a sporting career there waiting and Brad has turned his life around through enthusiasm, passion and commitment. It was golf that gave him his new sporting outlook. Ten years after the horrific accident, Brad met fellow amputee Jeff Nicholas, who introduced him to competitive golf.[168] 'I met Jeff just by chance really. I just typed in amputee golf one time on the computer which took me to a website. That's how we got in contact and that's when I took up the sport.' Brad competed for the first time at the 2005 NSW Amputee Open. He followed that up with a trip to Japan to compete in the Japan Open Golf Championship for disabled people. He finished third in the tournament, which was a major achievement:

> I always try hard, but I didn't expect to do so well. I just wanted to go over and get my first international tournament out of the way and gain some experience. The first round, I didn't go too well. I was near the bottom but then I came back in the second round which put me up in third spot... Some of the golfers I competed against have been playing for 20 or 30 years, so to only have played for two years and to finish third was great.[169]

However, Brad admitted that for a long time he did not cope after the accident:

> I was drinking and I went through a long depression. It's been 10 years, but when I knew that I was going to have a daughter, I started to think I should do something about my life and get out of the habit of just drinking all the time. So, I pulled into line and started playing golf.[170]

Brad was looking to the future and keen on taking his game to another level. 'When you get out on the golf course, nothing else matters but hitting the ball.

---

168 *Deadly Vibe,* 30 November 2007; https://deadlyvibe.com.au/2007/11/bradley-hardman/

169 Ibid.

170 *Deadly Vibe,* 30 November 2007; https://deadlyvibe.com.au/2007/11/bradley-hardman/

Anything could happen in my life but when I'm out there, I'm just free.'[171]

In 2010, Brad captured the Australian Open Amputee Golf Championship and went on to run boxing training programs for young Indigenous kids from Maroubra and La Perouse. Through his own life experiences, he wanted to guide and advise the kids: 'I talk to them about what they want in life. I try to mentor these kids and help them become better people in the future.'[172] The message from Brad is there for young Aboriginal kids – make the right choices in life and shoot for the stars.

Norm Hodge

Victorian Aboriginal golfer Norm Hodge made history in 1999 when he was selected a member of the first Aboriginal golf team to tour overseas. He was a part of the Victorian Aboriginal Golf Association team. It was noted that the first two days of the tour would be a 72-hole competition against Māori and Samoan teams. The other two days would be 36-hole events against individual New Zealand clubs. All the events would be played in Auckland. The team of sixteen were selected from the association's fortnightly competitions across the State. Having only taken up the game three years earlier, Norm was surprised but very excited about his selection on the tour:

> It's an honour. I nearly fell over when I found out [I was selected]. Kooris weren't involved in golf in my youth. They were not allowed on the course. It means we've come a long way to being able to play golf.[173]

Kevin "Sooty" Welsh

Kevin "Sooty" Welsh, a much respected Wayilwan ceramic artist, today makes pots and other pieces richly glazed with unique designs. The designs and

---

[171] Ibid.

[172] Ibid.

[173] *Riverine Herald (Echuca)*, 28 July 199: 20

markings are closely linked to Wayilwan culture and memories. "Sooty" was removed from his family as a young boy and taken far away from his country to an institution. The suffering inflicted by child removal policies and institutional abuse has intergenerational impacts, and the trauma experienced during childhood has been carried by many into adult life. "Sooty" is a member of the group recognised today as the 'Stolen Generations'. Dr Mariko Smith from the Australian Museum in Sydney noted that his art practice is inspired by his Wayilwan heritage and the traditional carvings on trees but also makes marks that represent the scars that were inflicted upon him as a young boy in institutions where he was placed.[174]

Eventually, he was lucky to return to his community and family. He reflected that as a young man, he worked on golf courses including the Australian Golf Club in Sydney back in the 1980s for around 10 years. He recalled that he had worked on a couple of golf courses, but the Australian was by far 'the best one I've worked on. We were able to play it on Tuesday arvo after work.'[175] He also worked at the Kooralbyn Valley and Bonnie Doon Golf Clubs.

He reminisced about the big skins' game played at the Australian Golf Course in 1985 and looking across to the 18th green where half a million dollars in cash was sitting in the middle. It was the first major skins' tournament in Australia, and they were playing for $10,000 a hole. He remembered that he used to mow the fairways on a $150 machine. That tournament was won by Greg Norman, who collected the largest sum of $144,000, and the playing field included Jack Nicklaus, Tom Watson and Seve Ballesteros.

May Chalker

May Chalker is an inductee of the Aboriginal Sports Hall of Fame. She was born in the town of Wagin in Western Australia and one of ten children. In a wheat farming district where there was not a lot to do around the town, she took up

---

[174] https://australian.museum/learn/first-nations/Scarred-Ancestral-Vase/

[175] Personal correspondence with Kevin "Sooty" Welsh 30 November 2023.

May Chalker, a top class Aboriginal golfer.
(Photo: The late Colin Katz, Paul Tatz and the Aboriginal Sports Hall of Fame).

golf, playing with just four battered men's clubs, a 3 iron, 7 iron, a driver and a putter. She moved to Perth in 1970 and continued with her passion for golf, winning the 1976 Country Championship. In 1982, she won the State singles title and captained the State side that year. She would go on to represent Western Australia for six years, including captaining the State team twice. In 1979, she won the State mixed fourball title with her son Mark, later the first Aboriginal professional golfer. In 1980, her daughter Marion played in the State junior team while May was playing in the State senior team at the same time. May was also a State team selector for two years.[176]

---

[176] Tatz, C (1995) Obstacle Race, UNSW Press, Sydney: 279; Tatz, C & Tatz, P (2000) *Black Gold*, Aboriginal Studies Press: 66; Tatz, C & Tatz, P (2018) *Black Pearls, Aboriginal Studies Press, Canberra*: 32.

Skye Lampton

A more recent Aboriginal woman golfer who has captured some attention is 29-year-old Dagoman, Wardaman and Gurindji golfer Skye Lampton. Skye has had a remarkable and unlikely journey to the golf course. She came into the game purely by accident as she grew up in Katherine, before going to high school in Darwin.[177] Next, she applied for an advertised position as an au pair in the United States. First, she was based in Arizona before moving to Maryland. In 2015, while working in Annapolis, Maryland, and feeling a little bored, Skye and a friend were driving around when they spotted a driving range. They decided to give it a try and the first ball she hit flew off some 175 yards. She was hooked and was soon going to the range to hit balls two and three times a day, even taking the kids she was caring for along with her at times. She met wonderful and kind people at the range who gifted her clubs, bags and a putter, and then took her along for a real game. Skye said she wanted to shoot her best score every time she went on a course. The game came naturally to her thanks to a sporting background that included playing softball, touch footy and netball in Australia, as well as indoor volleyball in America.

On returning home, Skye was working in Darwin for the government. At first, there was no time for golf until a friend invited her along to a driving range. It was while hitting balls there that a woman in the next bay asked, 'What's your handicap?' Skye replied, 'What's a handicap?'

The woman invited Skye along to be her partner in a nine-hole ambrose event at Darwin Golf Club with Skye given a handicap of 45. She parred six of the nine holes, and the pair won the event.[178] Skye then joined the Darwin Golf Club where she now plays on both Saturday and Sunday and fits in a game on Thursdays as it is a flexi half-day at work. She has since become one of the most successful female Aboriginal golfers in the history of the game in a very

---

177   Owen, P (2023) Skye's the Limit for Lampton, *Inside Golf*:10.

178   Owen, P (2023) Skye's the Limit for Lampton, *Inside Golf*, :10.

Rising star Skye Lampton.

short time. Skye won the National Aboriginal and Torres Strait Islander Golf Championship in Perth in 2022. In January 2023, Skye became the first Aboriginal woman and just the fifth woman to represent the Northern Territory at the Australian Amateur Championship at the New South Wales and St Michael's Golf Clubs.[179] She reflected, 'It was great. I couldn't have asked for a better group. The girls were lovely and the golf courses at New South Wales and St Michael's were beautiful. Unfortunately, I played terribly.'[180] She said she wanted to become an associate professional under Golf Australia's Membership Pathways Program.[181]

---

[179] Rolley, A (2023) Skye's the Limit, *Australian Golf Digest,* March: 25.

[180] Owen, P (2023) Skye's the Limit for Lampton, *Inside Golf,* :10.

[181] Owen, P (2023) Skye's the Limit for Lampton, *Inside Golf,* :10.

Ash Barty

Three-time Grand Slam singles tennis star Ash Barty, now retired from tennis and a recent mother, has a great love of golf and some have even spruiked a professional career on the golf course. Barty did make her sporting return on the golf course as a guest invited to the New Zealand Pro-Am Championship in

Three time grand slam tennis star Ash Barty loves her golf.

early 2024. She is a keen golfer who plays off a handicap of 4.[182] Barty sadly missed the cut for the weekend by just two shots and she made it clear that golf remains just a hobby.[183]

The National Aboriginal Golf Championship

Famous Aboriginal soldier, Captain Reg Saunders, was a very keen golfer and is recognised as the first Aboriginal member of Dunheved Golf Club in Western Sydney. Saunders played a role in establishing the first National Aboriginal Golf Championship. He had fought in both the Second World War and in Korea and is recognised as the first Aboriginal military officer. The first ever National Aboriginal Golf Championship was held at Dunheved in Western Sydney in 1979. The tournament was the brainchild of former AFL and Carlton star Syd Jackson and Bob Morgan, who at the time was working as the public relations officer for the Aboriginal Medical Service. They were soon joined and supported by Dunheved club captain Johnny Delaney, Dan Rose, Captain Reg Saunders and PGA members Ian Stanley and Kelvin Llewelyn. The first tournament was a raging success with a field of 40 competitors battling for the top honours.

Syd Jackson delivered on the seventh hole with a drive that registered 320 metres.[184] Syd remains as one of the great Aboriginal AFL players with Carlton in the 1960s and 1970's. Syd Jackson had the opportunity during his playing career to tee up on the golf course with Carlton supporter and golfing legend

182 www.foxsports.com.au/golf/golf-news-2024-ash-barty-sporting-comeback-at-the-new-zealand-open-why-did-she-retire-from-tennis/news-story/0e0c64d3d3840528f60e7300873904bc

183 www.news.com.au/sport/golf/ash-barty-misses-the-cut-in-her-return-to-competitive-sport-at-the-new-zealand-open/news-story/5aa7883e40ec07ccdc689f16331eaffb

184 *Australian Golf,* June 1979: 9

five team British Open champion Peter Thompson. 'Jackson and Thompson became friends and 'Thomo' invited him for a game of golf at Royal Melbourne. Jackson still remembers it with great affection for Thompson all these years later. "Imagine that? A black man on the first tee at Royal Melbourne he said. Jackson knew it was a powerful statement by the Open Champion all those years ago'.[185]

The winners of the inaugural National Aboriginal Golf Championship event were 'La Perouse legend Chooky Lester and Sonya (Scott) Hinkley'.[186] Golfers Kel Llewellyn and Ian Stanley attended to watch the tournament and ran some golf clinics for the players. The tournament was sponsored by 'Spalding, Niblick, Dunlop-Slazenger, and Ansett.'[187] Llewellyn was glowing in the potential of Aboriginal golf players:

> they should do well because they are so well coordinated. They have great rhythm, better than the average golfer, and they haven't got a white man's fear. They're all happy-go-lucky guys.[188]

Bob Morgan also highlighted the historical obstacles that Aboriginal players had to endure:

> It's only in the last five or 10 years that Aboriginals have taken a real interest in golf. They have found it difficult to get into certain clubs, but I think that is all changing now.[189]

The tournament was a great success, the weather was perfect, and Captain Reg Saunders was noted as one of the real personality players. It was declared that

---

185 Davis, M (2024) *Inside Golf,* Issue 230 December 2024: 22

186 https://alc.org.au/uncategorized/celebrating-40-years-at-the-nsw-aboriginal-golf-championship/

187 *Australian Golf,* June 1979: 9

188 Ibid.

189 Ibid.

the tournament would continue each year with representatives encouraged from across the nation. In 2019, the National Aboriginal Golf Championship celebrated its 40th year. The tournament returned to Dunheved Golf Club to honour the original event. Over one hundred players turned up. Over the years, the tournament has been played at some of the best courses in the country, including The Vines (WA), Horizons (NSW), Growling Frog (Vic), Bonville (NSW), Alice Springs (NT), Campbelltown (NSW) and Kennedy Bay (WA).[190] The event has always been an outstanding success and has fully vindicated the potential that organisers saw back in 1979.

---

[190] https://alc.org.au/uncategorized/celebrating-40-years-at-the-nsw-aboriginal-golf-championship/

Counting Coup – Native American Reflections and Comparatives

Counting coup is a Plains Indian tradition of winning prestige against an enemy in battle. It is a traditional way of showing bravery in the face of the enemy and intimidating him and hopefully persuading him to accept defeat without killing him.[191] I have already stated that I have had the great pleasure of playing alongside Indigenous colleagues and friends across the world. It is that coming together on the golf course that initiates much fun and laughter, as well as reflections upon global Indigenous historical experiences.

Reflecting upon those wonderful connections, I decided to look at the North American experience in a comparative sense for this book. I have been fortunate to have visited the United States many times over the past twenty-five years and had the opportunity to visit many Native American Centres within the university sector, as well as the Smithsonian National Museum of the American Indian in both New York and Washington D.C. But of equal if not greater importance has been the incredible experiences of visiting Native American communities in California, North Dakota, Florida, Texas, Nebraska, Arizona, New Mexico and Connecticut.

I have no hesitation in stating that for me, there is no greater comparative historical experience than that suffered in Australia and in North America

---

191 https://en.wikipedia.org/wiki/Counting_coup

On the course with Lakota brother Phillip DeLoria and brother Ray Kelly.

by the First Peoples through invasion, occupation, dispossession, cultural destruction, war and massacres, child removal and erasure from history. There have been some great Native American sports stars like Jim Thorpe, John Levis and Billy Mills, but like Aboriginal people, a lot of potential stars were overlooked and denied opportunities.[192] It is now recognised that there are 55 golf courses in the United States that are owned and operated by Native American tribal groups. Some of these courses have hosted PGA and LPGA events.[193]

I spent several years conducting a comparative historical study of Aboriginal Australian and Native American political activism in the early decades of the twentieth century. There are several connections between Aboriginal people and Native Americans. On reflection, Tasmanian Aboriginal Elder Jimmy

---

[192] Ibid.

[193] https://www.westrivereagle.com/articles/first-native-pro-golfer-gains-new-recognition-after-100-years/

Everett recalled that Aboriginal people in Tasmania and nationally looked overseas to international Indigenous experiences to try to understand and make sense of what was happening here in Australia, and to see if anything could be learned to help the Aboriginal struggle for sovereignty here.

Everett recalled fellow Tasmanian high-profile Aboriginal activist Michael Mansell sent him off overseas to meet with and offer support to the Mohawk leaders in Canada in 1989. It was reported that the Mohawk people were 'stockpiling weapons and food in readiness for war against the government in Quebec'.[194] The issue and escalation of tension was over the government's plan to develop a golf course on Mohawk land. The plan was for Jim to meet with television reporters on his arrival and gain a press badge that would allow him access to a place called Oka, just outside Montreal.[195]

In Montreal, Jim found his hotel and met an Australian television journalist who provided his press badge and took him to meet the Mohawks. Jim was introduced to Leader John Cree who explained the reason why his community was fighting to protect their land. Jim stayed at the protest site for ten days while the Mohawks and their supporters organised a protest march at the small town of Oka. Jim was taken along to be a guest speaker, and he recalled the heavy military presence. The protest marchers were flanked by soldiers on all sides with rifles and weapons at the ready. Jim reflected that at times only a couple of feet separated the soldiers from the protest marchers. The marchers eventually moved on to a large paddock area where a stage had been erected, and speeches had begun. Jim stepped forward and delivered a message of support from Aboriginal people in Australia in their fight to protect their land and to end government interference and police intimidation.[196]

In 2019, it was noted that tensions were again rising between the

194 Everett, J (2023) Learning to Understand: my life story to Pakana philosophy, Master of History Thesis, University of Tasmania: 89-91.

195 Ibid.

196 Everett, J (2023) Learning to Understand: my life story to Pakana philosophy, Master of History Thesis, University of Tasmania: 89-91.

Kanien'kéha:ka (Mohawk) of Kanehsatàke and the Québec municipality of Oka. A report recalled that back in 1990, there was a major conflict at Oka where the government used 2,500 military troops to end a 78-day protest by the Mohawks to protect a burial site that was under threat due to the planned expansion of a golf course and construction of luxury condominiums. The Quebec government had initially sent in the provincial police, but when a police officer was shot and killed during the siege of the Mohawk blockade, the military was brought in. The 1990 conflict ended in a stalemate as development was stopped, but the land was not returned to the Mohawk people. Prime Minister Justin Trudeau was called upon by the Mohawk community to again stop development on the unceded land in 2019. The land in question had been at the heart of Mohawk demands for over three hundred years. Since 'the 17th century Mohawks have attempted by all means – from petitions and land claims to blockades – to have their land returned'.[197]

Back in 1990, the blocking of the development at Oka by the Mohawk people played a major role in the Canadian Federal government establishing a Royal Commission on Aboriginal Peoples in 1991 to improve relations with Indigenous peoples across the country.[198]

Russell Means and the AIM

In the United States in the 1970s, the rise of the American Indian Movement (AIM) and Red Power was another major inspiration to young Aboriginal activists in Australia. The occupation of Alcatraz in 1971, organising the march on Washington known as the Trail of Broken Treaties in 1972 and the Siege at Wounded Knee in 1973 saw the AIM gain international coverage and awareness. The AIM had several articulate, charismatic and courageous political

---

[197] Carleton, S (2019) The Legacy of Oka in an era of supposed reconciliation, *The Conversation*, 25 September 2019.

[198] Ibid.

Russell Means and Gary Foley, University of South Australia in 2010.

leaders that included Dennis Banks, Clyde Bellecourt, Vernon Bellecourt and Russell Means.

Russell Means was regarded alongside Dennis Banks as one of the greatest Indian leaders since Sitting Bull and Crazy Horse. He was unquestionably a man incredibly proud of his heritage and community of Pine Ridge. Russell Means would survive several attempts on his life. He was wanted on six warrants in two States, and he was convicted of involvement in a 1974 riot during a clash between the police and Indian activists outside a Sioux Falls courthouse. He served a year in a state prison where he was stabbed by another inmate. Means also survived several gunshots – one in the abdomen fired during a scuffle with an Indian Affairs' police officer in North Dakota in 1975, one that grazed his forehead in what he called a drive-by assassination attempt on the Rosebud Indian Reservation in South Dakota in 1975, and one in the chest fired by another would-be assassin on another South Dakota Reservation in 1976.

Means would later become a recognised actor and played major roles in the film *Last of the Mohicans* and the animated film *Pocahontas*. He visited Australia and was introduced to one of our own legendary activists, Gary Foley. Foley had no hesitation in stating it was such a great honour to be introduced to one of his own personal heroes in the struggle for Indigenous rights.

Russell Means also brings us to another golfing connection. During the trial at Sioux Falls, there was a recess period, and Means was joined by three carloads of AIM members. They headed up Highway 83 to attend a party at Mission, South Dakota. Just outside of town, the group stopped outside the Mission Golf Club and Resort. Means and the other AIM members had been informed that the golf club had a strict whites-only policy, and no Indians were allowed into the club.

In his autobiography, Russell Means states that the group were hungry and decided to test the club's policy. They were confronted by the club manager and told to leave, or he would call the police. The AIM group said, 'Go ahead'. The manager went on to call the Mission town police, having no idea that because the Mission Golf Club was sitting on an Indian reservation that the police had absolutely no jurisdiction. Means recalled that the police arrived: 'Tom Rhoads, Mission's redheaded chief of police, and Ron Haukaas, a light skinned breed – Rhoads immediately drew his gun, put it to my head, and said I was under arrest. I slapped his arm away and punched him out. Haukaas went for his gun, but my friend Kenny Kane laid him out.'[199] The AIM members had them on the run and they chased all the police and whites out of the building.

Several of the AIM members went downstairs and emptied several of the illegal poker machines. Outside several more AIM members trashed the police car. One of the AIM members Harvey Kills in Water was smashing the red light on the police car when he was thought to be accidentally shot in the head. Means revealed that the AIM member responsible for the shooting was later discovered to be an FBI informer. Means and the others rushed Harvey to

---

[199] Means, R (1995) *Where White Men Fear to Tread*, St Martin's Press, New York: 320.

hospital where he recovered. Along with others, Means faced court for the Mission Golf Club fight. Appearing before Judge Merhige, Means represented himself. He recalled of the trial, 'like many others on the assembly line of injustice, ours was very quick. At least our judge was a fair man, although he indulged in little contemplation. I argued that the Mission cops had no jurisdiction on the reservation' and had no authority. Merhige agreed and considered the whole incident 'nothing more than a barroom brawl'.[200] The judge threw out the eight felony charges and found the AIM members each guilty of simple assault. Means was sentenced to thirty days in jail.

Golfers of the Flower Moon

American film-maker Martin Scorsese's recent 2023 epic and traumatic film *Killers of the Flower Moon* delivered the disturbing story of the Oklahoma Osage Indians during the 1920s. In the film there is even a short clip of Osage golfers belting balls. After oil was discovered on Osage Reservation land in the 1920s, they were regarded as the richest per capita people in the world. The story reveals the wealth including cars, property, chauffeurs, homes and the dress of the Osage. Then one by one, they began to be murdered. Little attention was given to their sporting interests, including golf.

However, the Osage interest in golf predates the discovery of oil on their lands. In fact, the Osage believed that golf provided a way for their people 'to connect to the land'.[201] As Wagner revealed, money and cash draws out the vilest of human beings and the 'Osage Nation's experience with sudden wealth in the 1920s proves this to a tragic fault: the oil wealth brought in every manner of murderous crook and criminal and conniver'.[202] While through David Grann's best-selling book and Scorsese's film we are aware of the horrors of the time, we

---

[200] Means, R (1995) *Where White Men Fear to Tread*, St Martin's Press, New York: 320.

[201] Wagner, M (2024) Osage Love of Golf Older Than Oil Rush, *ICT News – The Voice of Indigenous People throughout the America's*: 1.

[202] Ibid: 2.

Chief Bacon Rind.

Joe Mills.

were largely unaware that at the very time of the murders, 'Chief Bacon Rind and the Osage hired Perry Maxwell to build a nine-hole course in Pawhuska.'[203]

A rather sarcastic and racist article appeared in a 1929 article in *Golf Illustrated* in 1929 titled 'Osage Indians like Golf'. Writer Roy Buckingham drew attention to the fact that the very wealthy Osage Indians had built their own golf course. He argued that only fifty years before, these people were hunting buffalo or chasing 'after paleface topknots.'[204] But the discovery of oil had made these people rich beyond imaginations. He revealed they played the local courses at

---

[203] Wagner, M (2024) Osage Love of Golf Older Than Oil Rush, *ICT News – The Voice of Indigenous People throughout the America's*: 1.

[204] Buckingham, R (1929) Osage Indians Like Golf, *Golf Illustrated*: 26.

Arkansas City, Kansas, Pawhuska and Ponca City 'in the most correct golf clothes on the courses.'[205]

Buckingham argued that the attraction of the game to the Osage was the opportunity to gamble. It was revealed that the 'younger Osages voted golf a good game and found they were welcome to play at the clubs in the Indian country.'[206] They probably did not question that their welcome status was due to their incredible wealth. The Osage clearly loved the game, and it was a distraction from the brutalities beginning to mount against them. It was not until the FBI were brought in that the sickening conspiracies and war being waged against the Osage people and their wealth was exposed.

The Osage golf course sadly no longer remains, as Anthony Shackelford who runs the Prevention and Primary Treatment for the Osage Nation said: 'You drive by and don't even want to look over there. It's all gone to seed.'[207] People still look over to the ghostly remains of the course. Shackelford added: 'It's still there. I mean, the greens are, but it hasn't been used for golf in a long time.'[208]

Notah Begay III

There have been some outstanding Native American golfers, but none more so than Notah Begay III. Begay's grandfather was a Native American marine in WWII who famously became one of the famous 375 Navajo Indian "code talkers". Speaking in Navajo, they completely fooled the Japanese and German intelligence and played a major role in victories across the Pacific. The young Notah Begay III shot his golf career into prominence in 1999 when he won two tournaments as a rookie and then drained a 22-foot birdie putt to beat Mark Calcavecchia to win the Greater Hartford Open. It provided his second

---

205 Ibid.

206 Ibid.

207 Wagner, M (2024) Osage Love of Golf Older Than Oil Rush, *ICT News – Osage Love of Golf older than Oil Rush*: Pg.3

208 Ibid: 2

win of the year and in just eight days, he had won more than a million dollars.[209] He and Tiger Woods were at one time roommates at Stamford College.

Begay III is the first 'full-blooded' Native American on the PGA Tour, and he is half Navajo and Pueblo. He grew up on the Isleta Indian Reservation outside Albuquerque, New Mexico and he hung around a rough golf course called Ladera. He talked the club professional into letting him help around the course for free range balls. The eventual payoff was Begay III's graduation from Stanford University with a Bachelor of Economics degree. He would have to earn his place on the PGA Tour. He and Tiger Woods were recognised as the first minority players to be selected for the US Walker Cup team in 1995. In 2000, Begay III notched up four wins on the tour, second only to Tiger's nine victories.

Despite the outstanding start to his pro career, Begay III hit some speed bumps that stalled his progress. His name in Navajo means "Almost There", and that in some sense sums up his self-inflicted fall from the top. He was clearly a perfect role model for Indigenous kids and took on that role with genuine fervour in wanting to inspire them with possibilities. Sadly, his message was derailed through a drink-driving offence that saw him register twice the legal limit and jailed for a week (as he had an earlier conviction for drink-driving and smashing into another vehicle). On his release, he admitted that it had 'been an uphill battle. Getting arrested and spending time in jail was the lowest of the low, and I'm not going to take anything for granted anymore.'[210] However, Begay III was clearly embarrassed and feared his impact of enhancing 'the stereotypical image of the "drunken Indian" ... And he hasn't had a drink since the accident.'[211] He revealed later that 'I learned from those mistakes and a lot of times failure is what drives you to success down the road. I made a mistake; I served my time in jail and didn't try to sidestep it.'[212]

---

[209] https://www.irishtimes.com/sport/time-in-jail-made-a-golfer-of-notah-1.289730

[210] https://www.irishtimes.com/sport/time-in-jail-made-a-golfer-of-notah-1.289730

[211] Ibid.

[212] https://edition.cnn.com/2013/12/13/sport/golf/tiger-woods-notah-begay-health-golf/index.html

Sadly, debilitating back problems further upset his career, but he took on the role of providing better opportunities for Native American kids through his Foundation.[213] Begay III was not afraid to step forward and speak on Native American issues: 'historically speaking, communities that have endured genocide suffer from generational trauma which leads to social issues, poor education, poor health outcomes, high crime and lots of addiction. These are the problems of the Native American community, and we are at the very beginning of the fight.'[214] Begay III spoke of the success of his Foundation and the importance of sport to wellbeing: 'Something which started as simply golf and then soccer for kids is now an evidence-based health and wellness program.'[215] Begay III set up a charity golf tournament that has raised over $4 million and Tiger Woods has taken part to assist his old friend's Foundation and programs. Sadly, despite several attempted comebacks, his back problems put an end to his golf career at the top. He has gone on to become a much-respected media commentator on the Golf Channel and NBC Sports, even appearing on EA Sports Golf game as a commentator.

Ricky Fowler

One player who was happy to play in Notah Begay III's charity golf tournament was Ricky Fowler. Fowler, like Begay III, has Navajo heritage. Early in his career, Fowler was noted for his flamboyant dress and preference for orange-coloured clothes. Begay III enthused over Fowler: 'His grandmother has become friends with my father because they are both of Navajo descent. I became aware of what Ricky was doing from his high school days, and he has brought a lot of flair to

---

[213] The Notah Begay III (NB3) Foundation is a national, award-winning Native-led nonprofit leading the way to improve Native American children's health. Each day, thousands of Native youths wake up facing significant health challenges and barriers to living full lives. The good news is that most are preventable and together we are changing this reality.

[214] https://edition.cnn.com/2013/12/13/sport/golf/tiger-woods-notah-begay-health-golf/index.html

[215] https://edition.cnn.com/2013/12/13/sport/golf/tiger-woods-notah-begay-health-golf/index.html

the game. He is a very good-looking young man, with the colourful clothes, his unique swing, and he has created a lot of interest.'[216]

Fowler went on to make a huge impact on the golfing world with six wins on the PGA Tour, including the 2015 Players Championship. He has had to be a bridesmaid on four occasions in the majors, finishing second in the US Open and British Open in 2014, as well as a third placing in 2014 US PGA Championship. He was second in the 2018 US Masters at Augusta.

Fowler went into a slump after his near miss at the Masters and struggled for the next four seasons, at one point only just holding on to his Tour card. Then he went back to former swing coach Butch Harmon and his results improved dramatically, winning the Rocket Mortgage Classic in 2023, his first win since 2019.

Off the course, Fowler played a part in the documentary film *Basketball or Nothing,* acting as an executive producer on the 30-minute, six-part series that followed a basketball team and 'the hoop dreams of an Arizona town located in the heart of the Navajo Nation'. Fowler reflected that his 'grandma grew up on the reservation, and I've always wanted to be able to do more stuff with the native community'.[217] Despite his four-year slump in form at just 35 years of age, Ricky Fowler has plenty of time to fulfil his promise and talent in taking out a major tournament. He is one exciting golfer I like to watch and follow.

Oscar Bunn – The First Native Pro Golfer

Any historical history of Native American golf players begins with the Shinnecock/Montauk golfer Oscar Bunn. He was born on the Shinnecock Reservation on Long Island and went on to become a Shinnecock tribal trustee. He was a Caddie Hall of Fame inductee, a professional golfer and teacher, and

---

[216] Ibid.

[217] https://www.redlakenationnews.com/story/2019/10/15/sports/professional-golfer-rickie-fowler-explores-his-roots-with-basketball-or-nothing-a-look-at-hoop-dreams-within-the-navajo-nation/84082.html

woodcarving artist.²¹⁸ Bunn became the first Native American professional golfer in 1896 when he played in the second ever U.S. Open with his friend, African American golfer John Shippen.²¹⁹ The pair were initially challenged by a group of white golfers who tried to stop them taking part, but they were allowed to play. It was recorded that the first head of the United States Golf Association, Theodore Augustus Havemeyer, put down the player revolt by stating that if the other 'golfers didn't take up their irons, he'd simply run Bunn and Shippen out there to play by themselves.'²²⁰

Bunn was a great golfer and caddy and was initially inducted into the Caddie Hall of Fame in 2009 'for his work in making golf more inclusive'. Being born on the Shinnecock Reservation, he was in close vicinity growing up to the famous Shinnecock Hills Golf Club. The Shinnecock tribal group had provided most of the labour to construct the golf course in 1891 on tribal land.²²¹ Bunn, like many of the young Shinnecock youth, gained working opportunities as a caddy at the golf club and experience in playing the course.

His natural talent with a club saw him selected to represent Shinnecock Hills Golf Club at the U.S. Open in 1896. Bunn finished in twenty-first place and Shippen finished fifth. Shippen probably should have won the Open except his ball apparently finished in a wheel rut and he scored eleven on the thirteenth hole of the second and final round.²²² The two friends again appeared together at the 1901 U.S. Open at Roland Park in Baltimore. Bunn's fame as a golfer continued to grow and in 1901, he was interviewed in the *Brooklyn Daily Eagle* with a four-panel illustration titled, "Shinnecock Indian Expert Tells How Golf

218 https://www.westrivereagle.com/articles/first-native-pro-golfer-gains-new-recognition-after-100-years/

219 Ibid.

220 Ibid.

221 https://www.westrivereagle.com/articles/first-native-pro-golfer-gains-new-recognition-after-100-years/

222 Ibid.

Should Be Played".[223] He later married a Shinnecock woman, Mary Della, and they lived together on the reservation. He had plans to teach golf in South America and applied for a passport. However, in 1917 he sailed from New York but became sick in October that year and died. He was only 41 years of age.[224]

Treaty

There is one stark difference between the Aboriginal Australian and Native American historical experience. Treaties were signed with Indian Nations in the United States as opposed to no treaties in Australia at all. However, it may be argued that the treaties in the United States were not worth the paper they were signed on as many treaty promises were broken.

Yet despite the long-running historical lies and breaking of signed treaties, Native Americans still retain an option to carry evidence of a treaty to support their legal claims in court. Native American Nations have land and as we have seen with the Osage in the 1920s, land once thought worthless was in fact rich with oil. Today, many Indian Nations have set up casinos that have brought wealth and unprecedented opportunities. Some even include golf resorts. For example, the Oneida tribe of Wisconsin own and operate Thornberry Creek, regarded as far and away the best golf course in Wisconsin. The course 'is a world-class golf course that has played host to numerous PGA Tour events. Beyond the course, the tribe nurtures future talents through a robust junior golf program, contributing to some of the finest Native American golfers globally.'[225]

These are exciting Indigenous golfing developments. Sadly, we in Australia are not in such a position but hopefully some far-thinking golf clubs could introduce Indigenous scholarships and development programs that could gain government support and encourage our young kids into the game.

---

223 Ibid.

224 https://www.westrivereagle.com/articles/first-native-pro-golfer-gains-new-recognition-after-100-years/

225 https://www.hagginoaks.com/blog/inspiring-stories-of-native-american-golfers/

Another significant American golf course is Lake Isles in North Stonington, Connecticut. Celebrated golf architect Rees Jones 'designed and built 36 holes of golf that dance through what was and is now again Mashantucket Pequot tribal territory'.[226] In constructing the course, archaeological surveys were conducted and ensured that respect for sacred sites, seashell and turtle symbols were worked into the design.'[227] Rees Jones stated: 'We worked with the tribe considering their background and history and what was essential to them. We understood what was important to them and included that in our approach.'[228] The turtle is the spirit totem of the tribe, and the seashell a part of the rich ocean economy that the tribe thrived upon before European contact.'[229]

Several national studies in the United States have shown that 'casinos, entertainment venues and golf have reversed social and economic decline for tribes nationwide.'[230] Tribal spokeswoman Lori Porter was adamant that: 'Being able to provide jobs, housing, healthcare, pharmaceuticals, cultural and educational opportunities, and a secure community are among our biggest priorities as a tribe.'[231] She went on to state strongly: 'Tribal sovereignty is our highest priority. We work to ensure the Federal government upholds its obligations to tribes. It's critically important to maintain strong government to government relationships and educate state and Federal representatives on who we are and how well we contribute to Connecticut as well as to Indian country, wherever needed.'[232]

Rees Jones stated that golf has an important part to play in reparations and healing from the past through 'giving them the land to control their own

---

[226] https://www.golfcoursearchitecture.net/content/golf-reparations-and-native-american-heritage

[227] Ibid.

[228] Ibid.

[229] https://www.golfcoursearchitecture.net/content/golf-reparations-and-native-american-heritage

[230] Ibid.

[231] Ibid.

[232] Ibid.

destinies'.[233] Mark Wagner concluded that 'the resurgence of the Mashantucket-Pequot Tribe is a shining example. That the game of golf has aided in the process is not a surprise to historians of a sport which, by its nature, requires truth telling, humility and a love of the land.'[234]

While we do not have treaties or casinos to broker our independence and futures in Australia, there may be possibilities through Land Rights and Native Title to explore opportunities to establish partnerships through the construction of golf resorts on Aboriginal land with long-term leases that ensure we retain land ownership. This would provide hospitality, tourism, golf course maintenance and playing, and other training opportunities.

Like our NSW Indigenous and National Indigenous golf championships, Native Americans also take part in Indigenous golf championships in the United States. It is clear they also enjoy the banter, fun and camaraderie throughout these events. Indian golfer Rob McDonald recalled being interviewed and the reporter 'couldn't stop laughing when it came up that I really enjoyed the Indian golf tournaments... It was as if picturing loin-clad warriors with war paint and spears trying to hit a ball out of a sand trap.'[235]

He went on to reveal that: 'For many, golf conjures up images of aristocratic society with snobby country clubs, servants and cranky old men.'[236] But this is far removed from the Indian experience. In 2024, one of the largest American Indian golf tournaments returned to Indian Canyon Golf Course in Spokane in Washington. In 2023, the tournament had attracted 165 Indian golfers. McDonald related the diversity among the players, including 'The classic Indian teasing [that] isn't captured in any textbook I've found... Office administrators... politicians, health officials ride with forestry workers. Some operate heavy equipment or work construction. Some are fighting to change Federal policy on

[233] Ibid.

[234] Ibid.

[235] https://www.spokesman.com/stories/2004/may/28/history-forges-the-link-between-golf-and-indians/

[236] Ibid.

water rights.'[237] It was fun not knowing who you might be paired with on the course, including one time a tribal leader and another year, 'I was paired with an Indian doctor who gently reminded me it's important to work off excess blood sugars through simple exercise. As American Indians, we're all dealing with a family history of diabetes.'[238]

McDonald closed his article with an important message to white golfers who come to Spokane 'to play the great local course – know the history of the land they walk. History is what makes us who we are today.'[239]

The similarity in experience of the Indian and Aboriginal golf championships are striking, as is the message to get out to mainstream golf courses and to respectfully recognise and acknowledge the Indigenous lands upon which they sit.

[237] https://www.spokesman.com/stories/2004/may/28/history-forges-the-link-between-golf-and-indians/

[238] https://www.spokesman.com/stories/2004/may/28/history-forges-the-link-between-golf-and-indians/

[239] Ibid.

Oral Memories and Stories

This chapter provides the opportunity for a small number of Aboriginal golfers to provide their insight and perspectives on the game of golf. They reveal the opportunities the game has provided as well as the history of denied access. They celebrate the fun, camaraderie and joy that Aboriginal people have experienced in playing the game. Of course, there is advice and encouragement for greater Aboriginal involvement and ways and means to achieve that.

Johnny 'J.D.' Delaney

J.D. is a Gamilaroi man from Burra Bee Dee Mission near Coonabarabran. His family fled 'the mish' in the mid-1930s when he was about five to escape the police 'taking us kids'. The family caught a goods train to Sydney and headed to the promised land of Redfern.

The first game of golf he ever played was when he was a married man living in Caroline Street, Redfern. A white friend, Bobby Tasker, had called by and asked him to come and have a game. They went to Moore Park on ANZAC Parade. J.D. had never played golf before. Bobby said he could use his brother's clubs in the back of the car, but they were left-handed clubs. He still managed to score 107 off the stick using them. Next day, he went straight down to Mick Simmons Sports Store, and 'it was ten bob down and ten bob a week. I bought a 3-wood, 3, 5 and 7-iron and a putter and some cheap balls. I've been at it ever since.'

Looking back, he said: 'Moore Park seemed to be the mecca for blackfellas wanting to play the game. They are trying to change it today into a nine-hole

John Maynard and Johnny Delaney after a round at Dunheved Golf club in late 1923 and doing an interview.

golf course. No doubt about it, a lot of us can say that we had our first game at Moore Park.'

J.D. reflected: 'When we became aware of the game. It's one game, then it's a personal challenge. I think it's the personal challenge and the personal camaraderie – you aren't out there trying to punch the piss out of someone.'

He joined Dunheved Golf Club in 1969. It was '$31 for a yearly membership. I had been to the TAB and scored a daily double and I joined up. I have served on the board, been club captain and they gave me a life membership.' The start of the national Aboriginal golf championship 'was due to the Carlton Aussie Rules legend Syd Jackson getting in touch with Bob Morgan and Danny Rose to see if they could get a club to host a national Aboriginal golf championship.' J.D. put the idea to the Dunheved Golf Club, and they jumped at it. The 'great army Captain, Reg Saunders, did all the spruiking. The board approved it immediately.' It was sanctioned by the Australian PGA and the NSW Golf Association, and the Aboriginal Medical Service supported it.

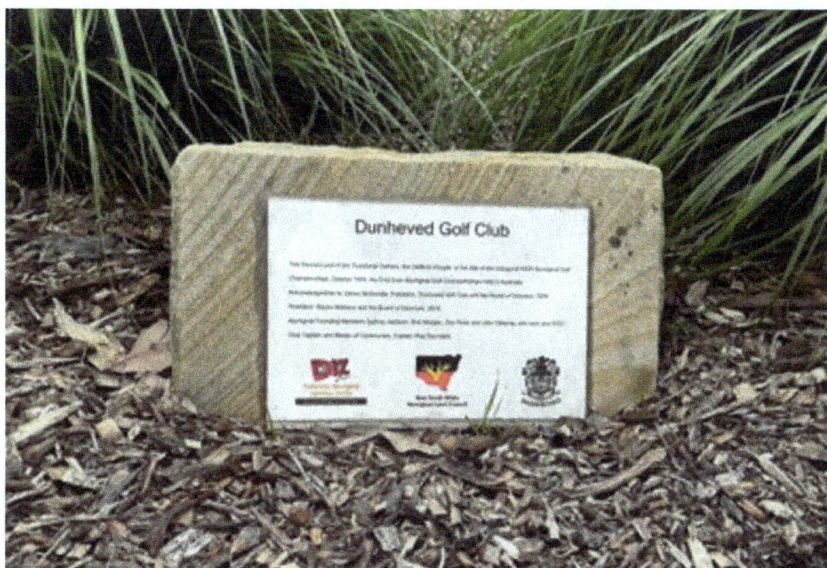

The marker at Dunheved Golf Club western Sydney to mark the First National Aboriginal Golf Championship in 1979.

Johnny Delany got his handicap down to four: 'I used to hit a hundred balls before I started. I got quite competent with the game and if I hit 78 or 79, I would get the shits. I played A and B grade pennants and had a long association with the Dunheved Golf Club.'

Johnny looks back on his years playing the game as some of the best moments of his life. He encouraged a lot of blackfellas into the game and club. 'It's been a really enjoyable association. I only ever encountered one bit of racism here, just one fellow. In the past, I would have just dropped him. But not worth worrying about. It's all about encouraging our people into the game and the need to start swinging a golf club before they can walk, just like Tiger Woods.

J.D. caddied before he even played the game. 'It was some amateur championship at Royal Sydney and a mate of mine said, "can you come out and caddy for this rich South African guy". He was a nice bloke and even invited us in for a drink at Royal Sydney, but we had to inform him that we could not go into the club for a drink. He commented that "it's as bad as back home".

Johnny Delaney

He said, "where do you drink then?" and we said, "the Eveleigh [pub] back at Redfern". He grabbed us a cab and drove back to Redfern with us. He came back with us every day and shouted all the brothers in the pub.' The South African told us what a great supporter for black people back in South Africa Gary Player was and that he had a black caddy.'

It was around this time that Gary Player was to appear in one of the big

Australian tournaments in Sydney and that there was talk of university students and Aboriginal protests being organised against him. J.D. 'spoke to Paul Coe and said this is the wrong bloke to protest against. He supports blackfellas.' Anyway, nothing happened as far as any Aboriginal protest was concerned. But groups of non-Indigenous demonstrators heckled and harassed the great South African player, and a slogan 'Racist Go Home' was painted on one of the greens.

J.D. also spoke of spirituality and burial sites on golf courses. A white fellow working for the department was sent on leave at Moree and J.D. was sent up to relieve him. He had family to stay with and he decided to go and play a round of golf on his day off. 'Everything was ok until I reached this par-3 hole. I suddenly felt really unwell and had to sit down. I thought I was having a stroke or something. I couldn't go on and had to go back home. I still can't explain it. There was at one point a big shit fight out there years ago as they would not let blackfellas on the course.' I was telling Aunty about what had happened, and she said, 'Do you know my boy, a lot of your family are buried in that spot.'

J.D. revealed that in NSW there were three Aboriginal golf club captains. Billy Harrison down on the South Coast, Bill Kennedy at Walgett and himself at Dunheved in Western Sydney. That is a sign of 'how things have changed for the better. I like to encourage as many of our people, particularly the young, to get into golf. The Jack Newton Junior Golf program has been very supportive. I was also involved with David Liddiard with the "Searching for an Aboriginal Tiger program.'

J.D. believes golf is the greatest recreational sport and a great social sport as well. Dunheved Golf Club has been like a family to him, and it's been like that all the way back to 1969. Membership at the club created so many opportunities to employ our mob. J.D. had people employed behind the bar. Just being a member of a golf club provides job opportunities. It's a good place to initiate things. 'We had captains of industry sitting around the table and it does open the way for people.'[240]

---

240   John Maynard interview with Johnny Delaney at Dunheved Golf Club, 28 November 2023.

Nathan Towney

Nathan Towney is a proud Wiradjuri man from Wellington in western NSW. He is the Indigenous pro vice-chancellor at the University of Newcastle and director of the Wollotuka Institute.

Nathan has no hesitation in stating that his earliest memories of golf are of being freezing cold out at Wello [Wellington], having the beanie and gloves on and going out with his dad to play golf. 'There was a Sunday morning comp that dad loved to play in. It was called the Diggers Comp, and it was run by the Wellington RSL club. I'd get my packet of chips and a drink, and I would sit up on dad's cart and he would wheel me around while he played. I got to connect with him and his mates. I had little cut-down sticks and every now and then when I could feel my fingers and had warmed up, I would get down and have a few hits. Over the years, I progressed from not just having informal whacks but playing in the comps and joined the club.'

'I was 12 or 14 when I won the club B Grade Championship and then won the Foursome Championship with Les McCarthy, one of dad's old mates, when I was 14 or 15. That was probably when I started to get serious about footy and I made the State under-15 team, and my golf probably suffered from that. If I had my time over again, I would probably have given the footy away and stuck to the golf. Prior to that, we had a bus load of junior golfers from Wellington riding around right across central western NSW playing in the Jack Newton Junior program. There were quite a lot of young blackfellas in that program at the time.'

Nathan's dad was a plumber and then owned and operated his own security business in Wellington. As the police Aboriginal liaison officer, he was entrenched in the local community. He dealt with a lot of the business owners in the town and in some ways laid a platform for Aboriginal people in the town. 'I didn't really recall any other Aboriginal men playing golf other than dad until I was about twelve.' In terms of building a bridge and providing access in lots of different ways, Nathan's dad played a role, and golf was one of those areas that he helped to open.

The golf course is a unique setting and 'where else do you get to spend four or five hours with strangers or people that you may not normally spend time with?' asks Nathan. On a golf course you get that opportunity to 'get a true sense of someone's character and it develops a sense of trust and respect.' When Nathan and his wife moved to Sydney to pursue his football career, he joined the Cammeray Golf Club on the north shore. He became entrenched in the golf club. Looking back, he said 'it was when I was playing the most golf, and I did not realise how lucky I was.' Nathan was a member for a couple of years when they invited him to join the board of the golf club 'and that was my first introduction to governance, committees and boards.' It really did 'provide a platform to learn that stuff as well and it impacted on my professional career, and golf did impact in that way.'

Nathan Towney is adamant that national and local Aboriginal golf tournaments are important and have a positive impact. 'People come from everywhere. It's a real sense of community. From the moment you get there, you are laughing for four or five days. Taking the piss out of one another. It's like being with a big family.'

Nathan felt that racism is not something he has observed in connection with golf in a frequent sense, but he did 'remember his dad going off his head one time at Wello'. One of the young Aboriginal boys was a gun golfer, winning a lot of local championships. He was playing in the Wellington Club Championship. He had shot four under and was leading by a big margin and he was then informed by club officials that he was not eligible to play as his club membership had lapsed the day before the event. Nathan recalled that the junior fees at Wello were not a lot of money and to be just a day over! Nathan's father ripped into the club president and officials over the decision. Nathan and his father stormed out of the club, but the action had an immediate impact. Nathan recalls 'to the club's credit, they had a rethink and accepted his late fee, and he was awarded the club championship.'

Aboriginal people have such fun and laughter on the golf course. Nathan recalls many such moments where 'they are trying to put someone off their shot. If they are behind a tree or shaking over a putt, all the phone cameras come out.' He remembered one incident where a friend was behind a tree and hit his shot.

It cracked into the tree, shot back over his head, and landed in the golf cart. Each year, Nathan, two cousins and uncles head to Bonville. 'One of my uncles just has to look a bit uncomfortable over a shot and we start giggling and he is gone'.

Nathan is a great supporter of encouraging Aboriginal kids into the game. 'I am actually seeing even out at Wello a resurgence with young kids getting into the game and a real increase in young blackfellas picking up golf clubs.' He was nevertheless keen for golf clubs to focus on 'supporting our mob into the game and increasing Aboriginal participation and numbers in the game'. Nathan also supports the idea of being innovative and Aboriginal communities looking to be proactive. 'It is a common phrase that our people are land-rich but money-poor.' But potentially there are opportunities through the Land Rights Act and Native Title to go into partnerships with golf course development.

Nathan Towney is a keen follower of golf and watches the major tournaments on TV. His wife gave him a surprise 30th birthday present – a trip to Hawaii for the annual PGA Tournament of Champions at Kapalua Golf Club. Australian Geoff Ogilvie won the event, beating a field that included Phil Mickelson. Nathan has also attended the major Australian golf championships. He said his dad's favourite golfer was Greg Norman, so he also liked to watch Norman at his peak. 'Today, I like Cameron Smith with his short game and putting ability. Bubba Watson was another one who just did things out of the box. Tiger Woods of course has done things that no one else could achieve.'

Nathan also reflected that 'there is nothing better than to be out on a beautiful golf course. You are out on country – the birds, trees, bush native animals and reptiles. The serenity of it all. There is nothing better than to go for a walk on a great course.'[241]

Ray Kelly

Ray Kelly is a Dunghutti, Gumbaynggirr, Gamilaroi and Yuin man through his

---

241 John Maynard interview with Nathan Towney Newcastle, 19 July 2024

parents' family lines. Ray was born in Armidale at the Aboriginal reserve nicknamed 'Silver City'. He reflected that on one side of the reserve was the town garbage dump, and as kids they would scrounge and scavenge through the tip to see if they could find something useful. Occasionally, they would unearth some old golf clubs and a few balls that led them to peg out a mini golf course to belt the balls on and see if you could get around in under six. He recalled that they knew golf was a game. The greatest difficulty faced was in keeping balls, as kids wanted to belt the ball out of sight, and they would drive it into the bush. The very first terms Ray recalled learning in connection with the game were 'cacky hander' and 'par'.

The Kellys later moved to Grafton, and it was at 'South Grafton that the brothers and I used to play golf at the Grafton Golf Club. We would just jump over the fence and play a couple of holes. We weren't playing the game properly. If someone came along, we would jump off and then come back on to play a few more holes. We got to know the differences with the game.'

There were barriers to getting on a golf course, whether real or imagined, Ray reflected. 'We just never thought of going up and asking if we could have a game. But we just could not afford it. We did not have any money. It would have been wonderful if someone might have been able to help us.' Ray recalled that they did also scavenge for balls in the dams and bush and then sell them back to the golfers.

He moved to Newcastle when he was seventeen and never returned north to live, now considering Newcastle as his home. Over the years, he recalls there were several stalwarts and real legends of Aboriginal golf, including Johnny Delaney and Bob Morgan. 'Then some of us younger fellas stopped playing football we took to golf. Playing with brother Trev Patten and Joe Perry. We had big numbers playing in the local golf days back then and it is something I miss. The national championships were big and brought people together from all States and Territories, and it's on the golf course that you get to meet some of the real characters in our communities.'

'In this country, Greg Norman helped build an enormous profile of the game. The things he could do with a club and the length he could engender.

The zipping of balls back with spin. Jason Day is another one and he plays like a blackfella.' Ray has no hesitation in saying that his favourite current player is the Japanese Masters champion Hideki Matsuyama. 'I really love it when he is on the level of concentration. Of course, there is Tiger, and he is at the top of any tree. I watched him from when he was very young and the aura that surrounds him.'

Ray is adamant that racism is something he believes is largely absent from the golf course. 'You might get some feisty old members who want to move you along for playing too slow and they are probably just having a bad day. Golf is in a sense a gentleman's game and there is an element of truth in that. It is really about the game.' There is something about the game that brings out the best in people. It is a great space and the more people we have playing the game, the better. That is the gift of the game: 'When people need a hand, like, if you have an old set of clubs, give them to somebody.'

Ray has sound advice on encouraging more Aboriginal people into the game: 'I think it's around the profile. There has to be a strategy developed. I see the Federal government is giving a hell of a lot of money to the NRL. Maybe someone in the golfing space needs to speak to the government to initiate things to support some of our young kids into the game. Maybe we could have our own Tiger Woods.'

He feels that: 'Golf clubs could do more, but again, someone has to take up the initiative.' The golf club at Charlestown in Newcastle has land on its boundary owned by the Awabakal Land Council and Ray thought that maybe some development partnership could come out of that. He had no hesitation in stating that 'there are reasonable parcels of land owned by Aboriginal Land Councils across the State of NSW, so partnerships with a golf course and resort developer might be an option. The main aim for the Aboriginal communities is in providing social housing. But social housing won't pay the bills if you sell or lease land to a golf course developer with social housing around it.' He added: 'It goes to that initiative of doing for yourself instead of waiting for others. Any development has to be sustainable.'

Ray Kelly likes to watch golf and was keenly following the 2024 British Open at Royal Troon and really liked the par-3 "Postage Stamp" hole and the problems it can cause. He has played some top courses like The Lakes and New South Wales in Sydney, and he also thinks Newcastle is a top course. 'Newcastle is special, it's not far off the road to Nelson Bay and is close to the city. Wonderful wildlife, the wallabies and bird life of ducks and fowls.'

In thinking back over his years playing golf, Ray reflected: 'I think getting up early in the morning and getting to a course. Someone has the burgers on, and people are already starting to gee one another up. We turn a golf day into a big catch-up and tell stories.' He recalls playing a round with Jimmy Wright at Waratah Golf Club: 'Jim liked to go around in his golf cart, and I joined him in the cart. I drove a ball up onto a hill and he drove up, pulling up right next to the ball. There was no room to stand or swing the club. I said: "Jim, I can't hit the ball, you will have to go back and turn around and come back up." Jimmy Wright did so but was up against the ball on the other side with still no room to swing the club. I just looked at him and said: "Why don't we play it like polo and just swing from the cart."

Ray clearly has a problem with golf carts. On another occasion, he was playing a round at Bonville near Coffs Harbour with Stevie Blunden and again he had hit a ball up on another hill. Instead of letting him walk up the hill and hit the ball, Steve drove up it and Ray chipped back down onto the fairway. The hill was steep, and coming back down, the cart was moving a bit quick, and it spun sideways, spitting Ray out. 'I overextended my arm. I was buggered for the rest of the round.' But that is what golf is all about – the funny moments and the camaraderie.[242]

Joe Perry

Joe Perry's earliest memories of golf are illuminating. They involve the local golf course close to the Karuah Aboriginal Mission: 'I guess golf wasn't a game for blackfellas. It was a game for whitefellas that went on to the course to play.

---

[242] John Maynard interview with Ray Kelly, Newcastle 20 July 2024.

We weren't really welcome on the course. The fact is we were not welcome coming on from "the mish". People frowned upon us being there. But that didn't stop us, and we got on to play. We played quite a bit, had a few beers and a hit and giggle. Blackfellas really took to it; they embraced and loved the game. You are playing against yourself. It's not about beating anyone but also developing your mindset.'

The problem, Joe reflected, for us back in the day was that 'it's an expensive sport. You would be on an old set of clubs. Four of us would share the one bag of clubs and you weren't supposed to do that either. You had old, worn-out grips. The handles were old and worn and hard as a rock.'

Joe explained the attraction of golf to Aboriginal people: 'That's the whole point of golf – it is all about the camaraderie. Out with your mates, it's a hit and giggle. Taking the piss out of your mates and blackfellas love that at the best of times.' He recalled that there were so many funny incidents on the golf course – the continual taking the piss out of other players and the one-liners that blackfellas are famous for.

Joe has played all over Australia. Years ago, he and mates would travel down to La Perouse for the NAIDOC Week golf event at New South Wales, the attraction being that it was such a top course. Playing in the National Aboriginal and Torres Strait Islander Golf Championship, Joe felt that 'we'd get a lot of good young golfers coming through, but we needed that next step of support as there is a big gap between being a good golfer and a professional golfer. It's hard. You must get them young because that is when you learn the good habits. They can then learn to develop their swing. We'd just want to belt the thing.'

The reality as Joe sees it has 'a lot has to do with the parents. They are the ones who must encourage their kids, but it is so expensive for Aboriginal people. Parents would have to pay for the clubs and tuition.'

Joe confessed that he had not suffered personal experiences of racism on the golf course. In looking back, 'we were frowned upon trying to play golf at Karuah and elsewhere, but it was more of a middle and upper-class thing with people looking down upon us. It was a class thing.'

He believes there are certainly current opportunities for communities with land to do something connected with golf. In looking back, he recalled his late, great mate Trevor Patten and himself trying to get a golf course country club off the ground. The projected course was on land at Medowie, near where the present day Pacific Dunes course is today. 'We had approached the Department of Aboriginal Affairs to fund and support it.' But sadly, it fell through. This was a very positive and forward-thinking project that was years ahead of its time. Joe confessed that 'golf courses today are not making money, and most are struggling. That is why you need it to be combined as a resort location. It could then generate high employment for Aboriginal people.'

Of course, Joe indicated that, unlike Native Americans, we don't have treaties, and we can't build casinos. He indicated that Karuah Local Aboriginal Land Council 'holds a large amount of land, but we need some people with vision and action to get things moving.' They do hold some land close to the Hawks Nest Golf Club and at one point there was talk of a partnership to build accommodation on it alongside the golf course, but that came to nothing.

Joe has been a keen follower of the game and has attended the Australian Open to watch Tiger Woods. It has been so good following Tiger's career as 'a blackfella walking into a sport and just dominating it.'

He reflected on some of the top courses he has played and has no hesitation in stating that 'Newcastle golf course is a gun course, it's old school, a real classic. New South Wales in Sydney is another one.' Joe has played overseas in the United States and South Africa, including a course in Durban. He has also played several courses in Queensland and recalls a story he was told about Kerry Packer turning up at a course on the Gold Coast with four mates and being told that it was a private, member-only course. Packer said: 'How much is the membership?' The man replied '$50,000'. Packer's response: 'Good I'll take five.'

Joe's final words highlight the importance and appeal of golf: 'We have to encourage our kids to play as it is such a lucrative sport that offers so many opportunities. I just love it. The reality of golf is you rarely play well, as you know John [laughter]. And it's such a hard sport. You are just competing against yourself. I enjoy it so much out in the fresh air, on manicured fairways, the greenery, kangaroos on a lot of courses and the fun, the sledging, love it. I just laugh at some people who get angry when they are not playing well. You just have to enjoy the moments being out there.'[243]

---

243   John Maynard interview with Joe Perry, Newcastle 22 July 2024.

The Final Hole
– Where to From Here

It has just been such an enjoyable project to write this book. It has given me the opportunity to look back and reflect on my life and its intersection with golf across more than sixty years. The fun, pain, anxiety, enjoyment, frustration and exhilaration of this truly amazing game that truly captures all who pick up a club.

As with all my work over the past thirty years in researching and writing Aboriginal history, I like revealing aspects that are little known and filling the gaps and flaws in wider Australian history. I hope as part of this story I may have unravelled some of the mystery surrounding the attraction of Aboriginal people to the game of golf. It may well be in some way connected to the fact that we had traditional games that early settlers remarked resembled the game of golf. Clearly, Aboriginal Australia was also a sporting nation long before 1788. Aboriginal children were encouraged to play games that were about building fitness, endurance, agility and speed. Our people loved the competition of games and that it brought large groups and gatherings of people together to compete and celebrate sporting ability and success.

Of course, after 1788 and particularly into the late 19th and on into the 20th century, colour barriers and other forms of exclusion deprived many outstanding Aboriginal sporting talents the opportunity of taking part in Australian sporting pursuits. Golf had deeply entrenched class aspects that deprived Aboriginal people the opportunities to play. Of course, there was also the additional barrier of finance to overcome for golf clubs and membership, and then gaining admittance into a golf club. These were huge barriers to Aboriginal involvement.

Of course, from the 1960s onwards, greater opportunities for Aboriginal sporting talent saw the collapse of the colour barriers of exclusion and so many outstanding Aboriginal sporting stars burst through, including world boxing champion Lionel Rose, tennis stars Evonne Goolagong Cawley and Ash Barty, and athletic golden girl from the 2000 Sydney Olympic Games, Cathy Freeman. Both major codes of football – rugby league and Australian rules –took their time in breaking down access. However, over the last forty years it has been one long cavalcade of Aboriginal football stars dominating those codes. In the AFL, they include Doug Nicholls, Syd Jackson, Michael Long, Adam Goodes, Michael O'Loughlin and Buddy Franklin. In the NRL, there have been world-class players like Arthur Beetson, Eric Simms, Cliff Lyons, Greg Inglis, Johnathon Thurston and Latrell Mitchell, to name just a few.

Despite all the barriers and negativity, Aboriginal people have proven themselves to be resourceful in finding ways and means to overcome all obstacles to play the game of golf. Looking ahead, we need exciting initiatives to encourage our young kids onto the golf course from an early age. Both golf clubs and governments need to step up to support programs that encourage young Aboriginal kids into the game, and we as families and communities need to support their endeavours. We acknowledge that there may well be opportunities for Aboriginal communities through Land Rights and Native Title decisions to explore the potential of golf course and resort developers to partner with Aboriginal groups. This may provide employment opportunities not just within golf but also in hospitality and tourism. I certainly would like to see some of these initiatives undertaken, and a young Aboriginal golfer to be challenging at the top of the leaderboard in one of golf's majors soon.

References

Publications

Buckingham, R (1929) Osage Indians Like Golf, *Golf Illustrated:* 26.

Basedow, H (1925) *The Australian Aboriginal, F.W Preece and Sons, Adelaide*: 87

Booth, D and Tatz, C (2000) *One-Eyed – A View of Australian Sport,* Allen & Unwin, Sydney, pg. 63

Butlin, N (1983) *Our Original Aggression,* Allen & Unwin: 5

Browning, D (2023) Facebook Post, 1 June 2023.

Clayton W (1952) *Early Days of Port Stephens,*Edioted by Bennet, C.E., Dungog Chronicle:4

Curthoys, A, Koneshi, S & Ludewig, A (2022) *The Lives and Legacies of a Carceral Island: A Biographical History of Wadjemup/Rottnest Island,* Routledge, London: 370.

Davis, M (2024) *Inside Golf,* Issue 230 December 2024: 22

Dawson, R (1830) *The Present State of Australia,* Smith, Elder and Co, London: 68

Demos, L (2017) *Game of Privilege – An African American History of Golf,* The University of North Carolina Press, Chapel Hill: 205.

Eaton, C (2019) The Legacy of Oka in an era of supposed reconciliation, *The Conversation,* 25 September 2019.

Everett, J (2023) Learning to Understand: my life story to Pakana philosophy, Master of History Thesis, University of Tasmania: 89-91.

Estes, N (2019) *Our History is the Future,* Verso, New York: 249.

Fitzsimmons, 2019: 292

Frezier, M (1716) *Relation du Voyage de la Mer du Sud aux Côtes du Chily et du Pérou fait pendant les années 1712, 1713 et 1714*, Jean-Geoffroy Nyon, Paris

Hardman, B (2010) I Wouldn't Take My Leg Back, *Golf Digest,* 16 December 2010

Hardman, B (2007) *Deadly Vibe,* 30 November 2007

Kirsch, G.B (2007) Municipal Golf and Civil Rights in the United States, 1910-1965, *The Journal of African American History,* Vol. 92, No. 3 (Summer), pp.371-391; in Jackson, A, 2022, http://daily.jstor.org/daily-author/ashawnta-jackson/

Green, N & Aguiar, S (1997) *Far from Home – Aboriginal Prisoners of Rottnest Island 1838-1931,* Focus Education Services, Perth: 61

Gunson, N (1974) *Australian Reminiscences & Papers of L.E. Threlkeld,* Australian Institute of Aboriginal Studies, Canberra: 68

Means, R (1995) *Where White Men Fear to Tread,* St Martin's Press, New York: 320.

Maynard, J (2021) Nyuragil – playing the 'game'. In (Eds) Hokowhitu, Moreton-Robinson, A, Tuhiwai-Smith, L: Andersen, C & Larkin, S, *Routledge Handbook of Critical Indigenous Studies,* Abingdon, Oxon, Routledge: 555-565

Maynard, J (2014) *True Light and Shade – An Aboriginal Perspective of Joseph Lycett's Art,* National Library of Australia, Canberra.

Maynard, J (2024) *Fight for Liberty and Freedom*, Aboriginal Studies Press, Canberra: 59.

Millar, N.S. (2022) *Early Golf – Royal Myths and Ancient Histories*, Edinburgh University Press, Edinburgh, p. 174-175

Nadel-Klein, J, (1991) Picturing Aborigines: A Review Essay on After Two Hundred Years: Photographic Essays on Aboriginal and Islander Australians Today, in *Cultural Anthropology,* Volume 6, Issue 3, August 1991: 414-423.

Newberry, D (2023) *Inside Golf,* May: 14

Nugent, M (1987) *La Perouse – the place, the people and the sea,* Aboriginal Studies Press, Canberra.

Owen, P (2022) Play Golf Surrounded by Water, *Inside Golf,* August 2022, pp: 42-43.

Owen, P (2023) Skye's the Limit for Lampton, *Inside Golf,* :10.

Pollard, J (1964), *Gregory's Australian Guide to Golf,* Kenmure Press, Sydney: 117

Rhodes J (2018) *Cage of Ghosts*, Darkwood, Hong Kong: 132

Rolley, A (2023) Skye's the Limit, *Australian Golf Digest,* March: 25.

Seddon, G (1983) "The Rottnest Experience", *Journal of the Royal Society of Western Australia*, 66, pts 1 and 2: 34.

Spragg, I & Hopkinson, F (2017) *Remarkable Golf Courses,* Pavilion, London: 57

Tatz, C & Tatz, P (2018) *Black Pearls – The Aboriginal and Islander Sports Hall of Fame,* Aboriginal Studies Press, Canberra: 23

Taylor, P (1988) *After Two Hundred Years: Photographic Essays on Aboriginal and Islander Australians Today,* Aboriginal Studies Press, Canberra: 345

Utley, R.M (2004) *The Last Days of the Sioux Nation,* Yale University Press, New Haven: 40-43.

Wagner, M (2024) Osage Love of Golf Older Than Oil Rush, *ICT News – The Voice of Indigenous People throughout the America's*: 1.

Walker, A & Irish P (2023) *Golf on Gamay,* New South Wales Golf Club Foundation, Sydney: 11.

Newspapers & Periodicals

ABC News, 27 September 2013.

Adelaide Advertiser, 7 July 1928: 22

Argus (Melbourne), 18 November 1949: 5

Armidale Express and New England General Advertiser, 4 June 1937: 3

Australasian (Melbourne), 1944:30

Australian Golf, June 1979: 9

Barrier Miner (Broken Hill), 18 August 1923: 8

Brisbane Telegraph, 10 September 1949: 5

Canberra Times, 26 January 1993: 3

Daily Examiner (Grafton), 7 June 1937: 4

Daily News (Perth), 23 September 1953: 17

Daily Telegraph, 3 August 1947: 14

Daily Telegraph, 17 August 1947: 46

Daily Telegraph, 6 July 1941: 18

Daily Telegraph, 25 March, 1939

Daily Telegraph, 20 July 1947: 44

Daily Telegraph, 8 June 1941: 25

Daily Telegraph (Sydney), 29 November 1920: 6

Evening Journal (Adelaide) 1903: 1

Herald Sun, 29 October 2012

Kalgoorlie Miner, 5 August 1953: 8

Maitland Daily Mercury, 1 December 1900: 4

Nambucca Guardian News, 22 April 1983: 1

Nambucca Guardian News, 16 July 1982: 5

Newcastle Morning Herald and Miner's Advocate, 11 September 1933: 8

Newcastle Morning Herald, 11 May 1993

Newcastle Morning Herald, 10 October 1949: 1

Newcastle Sun, 4 June 1937: 5

New York Times, 26 January 2013

Nowra Leader, 1936: 4

Queensland Times (Ipswich), 21 December 1946: 7

Register News, Adelaide 1929: 7

Riverine Herald (Echuca), 28 July 199: 20

Singleton Argus, 30 November 1920: 2

Smith's Weekly, 1936: 4.

Sporting Globe (Melbourne), 12 October 1927: 10

Sydney Mail, 2 July 1930: 57

Sydney Mail and New South Wales Advertiser, 13 September 1905: 6

Sydney Morning Herald, 4 July 2020

Sydney Morning Herald, 4 December 2012

Sydney Morning Herald, 30 October 2012

Sydney Morning Herald, 27 November 2014

The Herald (Melbourne), 20 June 1936: 23

The Wallsend and Plattsburg Sun, 17 December 1890

The West Australian, 17 July 1936: 11

World's News (Sydney), 4 September 1935: 13

Oral Interviews and Personal Correspondence

Conversation with Gary Williams at Nambucca Heads 23 December 1923.

Interview with Uncle Rob Bryant via telephone 26 July 2022.

John Maynard interview with Johnny Delaney at Dunheved Golf Club, 28 November 2023.

John Maynard interview with Nathan Towney, Newcastle, 19 July 2024.

John Maynard interview with Ray Kelly, Newcastle 20 July 2024

John Maynard interview with Joe Perry, Newcastle 22 July 2024

Personal correspondence with Sooty Welsh 30 November 2023.

Vic Simms, 2021 Interview with Jai McCallister – A History of Aboriginal Rugby League in NSW – ABC Radio.

Websites

https://rathofarm.com/golf-course-history/

https://daily.jstor.org/fairness-on-the-fairway-public-golf-courses-and-civil-rights/

https://sahistoryhub.history.sa.gov.au/places/pirltawardli

https://www.keperragolf.com.au/cms/club/history/

https://www.smh.com.au/sport/golf/success-is-secondary-as-gardiner-blazes-
a-trail-20121203-2ar7w.html

https://www.smh.com.au/sport/golf/gardiner-takes-on-role-of-a-lifetime-
20121029-28fmz.html

https://www.nytimes.com/2013/01/27/sports/golf/an-australian-cuts-a-trail-
on-pga-tour.html

https://www.foxsports.com.au/golf/scott-gardiner-chipping-away-as-an-
aussie-nomad-golfer-with-his-family-half-the-world-away/news-
story/416b99f579357d54afdf72326d437546

https://www.smh.com.au/sport/golf/scott-gardiner-wins-car-with-hole-in-one-
at-the-australian-open-20141127-11v89z.html

https://pga.org.au/news/gardiner-trying-to-build-on-good-start/

https://deadlyvibe.com.au/2007/11/bradley-hardman/

https://australian.museum/learn/first-nations/Scarred-Ancestral-Vase/

https://www.foxsports.com.au/golf/golf-news-2024-ash-barty-sporting-
comeback-at-the-new-zealand-open-why-did-she-retire-from-tennis/
news-story/0e0c64d3d3840528f60e7300873904bc

https://www.news.com.au/sport/golf/ash-barty-misses-the-cut-in-her-return-
to-competitive-sport-at-the-new-zealand-open/news-story/5aa7883e40ec07
ccdc689f16331eaffb

https://alc.org.au/uncategorized/celebrating-40-years-at-the-nsw-aboriginal-
golf-championship/

https://en.wikipedia.org/wiki/Counting_coup

https://www.irishtimes.com/sport/time-in-jail-made-a-golfer-of-
notah-1.289730

https://edition.cnn.com/2013/12/13/sport/golf/tiger-woods-notah-begay-
health-golf/index.html

https://www.redlakenationnews.com/story/2019/10/15/sports/professional-
golfer-rickie-fowler-explores-his-roots-with-basketball-or-nothing-a-look-at-
hoop-dreams-within-the-navajo-nation/84082.html

https://www.westrivereagle.com/articles/first-native-pro-golfer-gains-new-recognition-after-100-years/

https://www.hagginoaks.com/blog/inspiring-stories-of-native-american-golfers/

https://www.golfcoursearchitecture.net/content/golf-reparations-and-native-american-heritage

https://www.spokesman.com/stories/2004/may/28/history-forges-the-link-between-golf-and-indians/

MORE REALLY GOOD BOOKS
FROM FAIR PLAY PUBLISHING

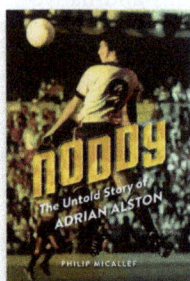

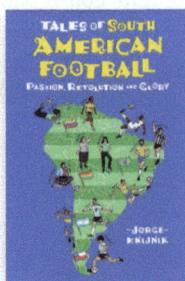

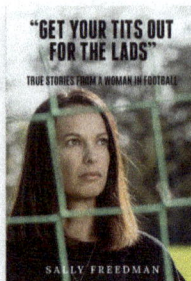

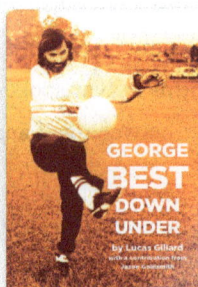

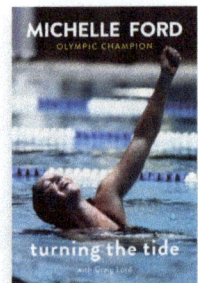

Available from fairplaypublishing.com.au/shop
and all good bookstores

FAIRPLAY
PUBLISHING

www.ingramcontent.com/pod-product-compliance
Lightning Source LLC
Chambersburg PA
CBHW070119030426
42335CB00016B/2201